"Once a photograph of the Earth, taken from outside, is available, once the sheer isolation of the Earth becomes plain, a new idea as powerful as any in history will be let loose."

—Fred Hoyle, Astronomer, 1948

"Man is beginning to inhabit a pretty small and overcrowded space ship, destination unknown, and the possibility that he may ruin it and himself in the process is by no means negligible."

—Kenneth Boulding, Economist, 1965

Committee on Geological Sciences

Robert E. Bergstrom
Head, Section of Groundwater Geology and
Geophysical Exploration
Illinois State Geological Survey, Urbana

John R. Borchert
Professor of Geography
University of Minnesota, Minneapolis

Ian Campbell, Chairman
President,
California Academy of Sciences San Francisco

Richard R. Doell
Geophysicist, Branch of Regional Geophysics *U.S.*
Geological Survey, Menlo Park, CA

Delos E. Flint
Chief Geologist
Freeport Minerals Company, New Orleans

LÉO F. LAPORTE, Principal author
Professor of Earth Sciences
University of California, Santa Cruz

John C. Maxwell, Vice Chairman
Professor of Geology
University of Texas at Austin

Clyde A. Wahrhaftig
Professor of Geomorphology
University of California at Berkeley

M. Gordon Wolman
Professor of Geography
The Johns Hopkins University

Cyrus Klingsberg, Executive Secretary
N.A.S.—N.R.C.

The Earth and Human Affairs

Committee on Geological Sciences
Division of Earth Sciences
National Research Council –
National Academy of Sciences

Canfield Press, San Francisco
A Department of Harper & Row, Publishers
New York · Evanston · San Francisco · London

THE EARTH AND HUMAN AFFAIRS
Copyright © 1972 by the National Academy of Sciences

Printed in the United States of America. All rights reserved. No part of this book may be used or reproduced in any manner whatsoever without written permission except in the case of brief quotations embodied in critical articles and reviews. However, this work may be reproduced in whole or in part for the official use of the U.S. Government on the condition that copyright notice is included with such official reproduction. For information address Harper & Row, Publishers, Inc., 10 East 53rd Street, New York, NY 10022.

International Standard Book Number: 0-06-385491-0 (cloth edition)

International Standard Book Number: 0-06-385490-2 (paper edition)

Library of Congress Catalog Card Number: 72-6804

72 73 74 75   10 9 8 7 6 5 4 3 2 1

To the memory of

William T. Pecora

*an early, effective, and enthusiastic advocate
of "the geologic perspective"*

foreword

The National Academy of Sciences has been concerned, throughout its history, with the application of science to increasing the well-being of humanity. Scientists generally have been enthusiastically responsive to this challenge, and this book represents the views of an eminent group of earth scientists on means of preserving our society by the most effective and wise use of our resources, including the earth itself. Additional light is shed upon many of the most challenging scientific and technical problems of our time. For this contribution, I am pleased, on behalf of the Academy, to express gratitude and appreciation to the members of the Committee on Geological Sciences.

Philip Handler
President
National Academy of Sciences

preface

For thousands of generations man has lived on the earth as just one animal species among many, making only limited demands on the environment as a hunter, fisherman, herdsman, or farmer. Within the present century, however, this relationship has changed drastically. With the growth of population—slowly at first, then explosively—that has accompanied more efficient farming and expanding technology, our species has achieved the capacity to alter our environment profoundly. The alteration is partly deliberate, as in the construction of reservoirs, canals, roads, and harbors. But in part the environmental impact is the inadvertent result of other activities, such as the pollution of the atmosphere by millions of automobiles, or the degradation of streams, lakes, and even oceans by industrial, municipal, and agricultural wastes.

Suddenly we have come to realize that we are capable of changing the face of the earth; that we are doing it at a rate often faster than the environment can absorb; and that we are, in fact, the overwhelmingly dominant force in the natural world. No wonder we are witnessing an outburst of public concern, usually mixed with confusion, indecision, and conflict, about goals, priorities, and tactics.

As geologists and as concerned citizens we have written this book with two fundamental truths in mind:
- This planet called Earth is the only suitable habitat we have.
- The earth's resources—living space, energy, and materials—are limited.

We realize that no single profession or group of people has *the* answer to our present environmental crisis. But we do believe that because all aspects of the environment are matters for concern, we, as students of whole earth processes and history, have a special responsibility to provide at least an introductory basis for understanding how the earth experiences change and how it evolves; the interactions between land and sea, between surface and interior, between process and product; and how these things relate to our activities on the earth. In particular, we provide a framework for understanding some of the basic natural controls of the environment, cite examples of our interaction with the environment, and conclude with suggestions on how we might restore and perpetuate an acceptable balance between our human needs and desires and the finite capacity of the earth to satisfy them.

L.F.L.

August 1972
Santa Cruz, California

contents

The Earth
and
Human Affairs

1

the good life:
what does it cost?

We live on the earth. Everything necessary to support life is available here and nowhere else in the solar system. And so we have to make the best use of what we have.

But do we? It appears that every use of the earth that is beneficial to humans exacts some environmental cost. The mere act of living pollutes and degrades the environment, as is obvious to anyone who has visited the village of even a primitive people. And when we demand something beyond simple existence—a steady food supply, heated or cooled homes, and mobility beyond the use of our feet—we require additional energy. This energy is generally supplied by burning some natural fuel, thereby adding more pollutants to the environment. In effect, the more we depart from a primitive way of life, the more we must expect and plan for pollution. Perhaps more significantly, many of the fuels and materials we use to improve our living standard, once expended, are irrecoverable. Their amount is limited, and in a relatively short time they will be exhausted.

In this chapter we discuss some aspects of environmental degradation and resource depletion caused by man's increasing desires for the "good life," with a few examples to illustrate the costs such a life implies.

ENERGY RESOURCES: CHALLENGE FOR TOMORROW

We are especially concerned here with the ever-increasing resources required to meet the energy needs we will have for many

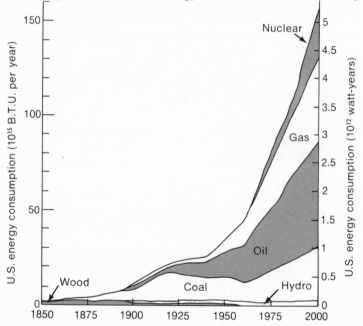

Figure 1-1. Graph showing the rapid increase of energy consumption in the United States from 1850 to the year 2000. Note the changing contribution of wood, coal, oil, and gas during the last century. Future projections of energy consumption indicate increasing reliance on nuclear power and coal, most of it strip-mined. SOURCE: C. Starr, *Scientific American,* Sept., 1971, p. 39.

centuries to come. Oil and natural gas, called fossil fuels because they come from the distilled fossilized remains of marine animals and plants millions of years old, are in limited supply. The resources of coal, another fossil fuel formed from the compacted plant debris of ancient swamps, are still very large; but the reserves of low-sulfur coal now required to meet stringent air pollution control specifications are much smaller. Energy available from atomic power is an addition to, and even substitute for, the energy presently obtained by burning fossil fuels.

Almost 95 percent of the power generated in the United States is now fueled by coal, oil, and natural gas (Figure 1-1). However, we have apparently reached the peak production of oil in the United States (and will in the world around the year 2000), and hereafter our national oil production will be declining. Peak production of coal and lignite (a brownish-black coal above the grade of peat but below soft, or bituminous, coal), which may again become the chief source of industrial energy with the eventual exhaustion of oil and gas, will be reached about three or four centuries from now and then decline rapidly. These are somewhat optimistic estimates of our fossil fuel reserves. Any extrapolation of the growth curves of our national energy use, *which doubles about every ten years,* indicates still more rapid depletion of our fossil fuels (Figure 1-2). Even very large discoveries of oil and gas will delay the time of exhaustion by only a decade or two.

We must anticipate, therefore, that the major part of the world's fossil fuels will be exhausted in the four- or five-century period from 1900 through about 2300 or 2400. "Exhausted" is the key word: *There will be no second crop.* Electric power generated from dams, hot springs, tides, and the sun may be greatly developed beyond present usage, but the total energy available from these sources will be far from adequate to replace the fossil fuels. Furthermore, hydroelectric sites are relatively short-lived because eventually sediment will fill in the reservoirs behind dams. In a similar manner, geothermal sources do not last indefinitely because the steam and heat that generate them will be depleted. Admittedly, there is always the possibility of a major technological advance that might significantly increase our energy resources. But until and unless there is such an advance, we must plan for the future in the context of our existing technology.

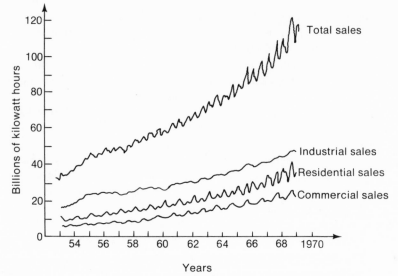

Figure 1-2. Monthly sales of electric utilities in the United States, 1953–1969, by consumer category. Note the seasonal fluctuations, particularly in residential sales, and the increasing peaks in summer use in recent years resulting from increased air-conditioning installations. SOURCE: H. E. Risser, *Power and the Environment—A Potential Crisis in Energy Supply* (Illinois State Geological Survey, Environmental Geology Notes, No. 40, December, 1970).

The electric power industry is beginning to turn to nuclear reactors to meet growing demands for power. Nearly all commercial power reactors being built today use a rare isotope of uranium, U^{235}, which must be separated from the much more common U^{238} by an elaborate refining process. Unfortunately, the known and probable reserves of mineable uranium ore will be depleted soon if the rapid growth of nuclear power plants using U^{235} continues over the next two decades or so. There is reason to believe, however, that before the year 2000 breeder reactors capable of burning the more common U^{238} and thorium 232 will be commercially available. If such a development occurs, nuclear power plants will provide power generation by using enormous quantities of uranium and thorium ore that are now far too low grade to be worth mining. Breeder reactors must be put into service soon because U^{235}, already in relatively short supply, is needed to fire up each breeder reactor when it begins operation.

RADIOACTIVE WASTES

Radioactive elements such as uranium and thorium disintegrate spontaneously at a constant rate; that is, they undergo spontaneous radioactive decay. In doing so, these elements form "daughter" elements, many of which are also radioactive. Certain elements may also absorb neutrons given off by radioactive elements during radioactive decay and change, by fission, into other elements. This process produces large amounts of heat, which of course is required for power generation. The radioactive by-products of this process, together with the unusable heat, are wastes that must be safely disposed of. The buildup of some waste products eventually will slow the fission process; so these extraneous elements must be removed chemically and the usable isotopes reformed into new fuel elements.

This chemical waste contains many long- to short-lived radioactive isotopes. Some, like strontium 90, cesium 137, and plutonium, are exceedingly dangerous to man and other organisms. Therefore, it is necessary to keep such radioactive elements out of the range of living systems until the radioactivity has decayed to harmless levels. For Sr^{90} and Ce^{137} the required isolation time is about 600 years. If plutonium accumulates in more than trace amounts, the waste must be isolated for about half a million years. Such lengthy time requirements add an entirely new dimension to waste disposal problems. Because of the enormous potential for affecting the natural environment, all activities relating to atomic energy are already more carefully monitored than any other technological activity. This monitoring is crucial; for if the atomic energy industry is to expand, the safety of waste-management programs must be adequate, not only for the well-being of our present generation but for all subsequent generations.

WASTE HEAT

Dangerous as they may be, radioactive wastes are not the only difficult waste problem associated with increasing energy production. For every kilowatt of electrical energy produced from the burning of fossil or atomic fuel, the equivalent of about 2 kilowatts of waste heat is produced. This waste heat must be disposed of within the natural environment. At present, the cheapest way to do this is to diffuse the heat in large amounts of cooling water, whose temperature is consequently raised approximately 5°–10°C. Because such large volumes of water are involved, the temperature range of a river, a lake, or coastal waters may be significantly changed by thermal discharge from large power plants.

The effect of such heated water on the natural waters receiving it depends on the temperature difference between the two and the rate at which the heat is dissipated to the atmosphere or mixed with the surrounding waters. Many aquatic organisms are physiologically sensitive to marked temperature fluctuations. Increased temperature also depletes the available oxygen of the receiving waters, which may be already in short supply owing to other forms of water pollution. Thus, the potential effect on the natural environment of growing thermal pollution may be profound. Although considerable research is currently being devoted to the study of these effects, little is known in detail about them.

Further compounding the problem is the fact that, at present rates of energy consumption in the United States, we will need in the early 1980s twice the energy now available and, in the early 1990s, four times as much. This means we will be producing four times more waste heat in the early 1990s than we do now. The difficulty in disposing of this greatly increased waste heat may be eased if somehow we can use it as an additional energy source. But unless that happens or unless we begin to reduce greatly our energy demands, we will have to exercise even greater care in the siting of power plants and in establishing criteria for using the nation's natural waters for thermal discharges. As required by the Environmental Protection Agency, we must thoroughly analyze the possible environmental effects at each site before any body of water receives waste heat from electrical power generation.

TRACE ELEMENTS AND HEALTH

In the early 1950s, adults and children in a Japanese fishing village sickened; almost half of them died. Even the seabirds and cats were afflicted. Chemical tests soon revealed that fish and shellfish taken from the local bay contained small quantities of mercury, and the concentrations of this toxic element were sufficiently high that the cumulative effect of eating the local seafood over a period of time was debilitating, if not fatal.

Health authorities around the world have subsequently made numerous analyses of foods from both fresh and salt waters, and of the waters themselves. They discovered that although mercury occurs naturally, some industrial processes also release small but significant amounts of mercury in their discharge waters. Even though the amounts are small and the mercury's state is initially insoluble, these "harmless" mercury compounds can be converted by bacteria in the natural environment into much more soluble and highly toxic organic compounds which subsequently enter the biosphere. And because living systems tend to take in mercury faster than they excrete it, mercury becomes concentrated in greater and greater amounts in animals at the top of the food chain. With the Japanese fishermen and their families, then, what apparently happened was that the mercuric oxides released into the bay by the local chemical plant were converted there into soluble organic mercuric compounds, and these compounds entered the food chain, becoming more and more concentrated up through the microscopic plants and animals, and the small fish and big fish that fed on them.

Continuing analyses of fish, particularly swordfish and tuna, reveal a number of samples in which the mercury content is well above the currently established maximum for human consumption. Analyses also have been made of fish preserved in museums; these fish lived when, presumably, industrial mercury discharge was much lower or even nonexistent. The remarkable thing is that some of these fish also have excessive mercury levels. The inevitable question thus arises: Have we been poisoning ourselves for centuries by eating these fish, or are the standards too low for permissible mercury content in food? We are now beginning to realize that we must ask the same kind of questions about many other elements present in trace amounts in our food and water, and in the air we breathe.

toxic effects

The toxic effects on humans of arsenic, cadmium, lead, mercury, selenium, and other metals have been documented, as has the increase of traces of these metals in the environment. There are definite correlations between certain trace elements in soils and the incidence of cancer, between calcium and tuberculosis, and between radioactive metals and congenital malformations. A relationship also exists between heart disease and the mineral content of drinking water.

Conversely, many elements that we previously considered only in terms of their toxicity are essential, in trace amounts, to the health of animals, to the point that their scarcity or absence can cause a variety of ailments. Interesting recent discoveries include the link between zinc deficiency and human dwarfism, between chromium deficiency and impaired glucose tolerance in humans, and between selenium deficiency and white-muscle disease in livestock. Moreover, certain trace metals are necessary for plant health. For example, the black, organic-rich soils of central Florida require the addition of several trace metals, including manganese, copper, zinc, and boron, before vegetables can be grown successfully.

Mortality and morbidity rates for many degenerative diseases appear to have patterns of geographic and geologic significance, but establishing a convincing link between a particular disease, or any other aspect of health, and the physical environment is exceedingly difficult. We need to know the pre-existing natural levels of metals in a given geologic setting before we can assess the potential dangers from additional metal contamination. To set standards for irrigation and drinking water, we must first determine the optimal concentration for each element so the metal content can be adjusted to the proper concentrations, and so beneficial elements will not be removed indiscriminately in water treatment and processing.

SALT: NECESSITY AND NEMESIS

Of the total volume of water on the earth, less than 3 percent is fresh water, and of that, only one-third is in rivers and lakes

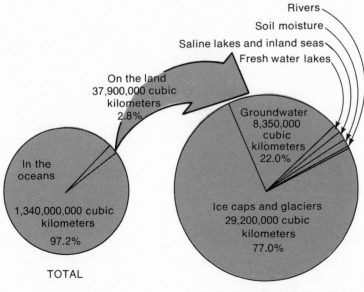

Figure 1-3. Distribution of water on the earth.

(Figure 1-3). Even this fresh water is not pure but carries with it varying amounts of dissolved mineral salts, one of which is common salt, sodium chloride. Fresh water is, of course, essential to life, yet the amount of good quality fresh water is small. Thus, the further contamination of existing sources of fresh water by human activities is a serious pollution problem, and occurs in many different ways.

surface salinization

In the United States the annual use of common salt for all purposes is about 300 pounds (136 kg) per person. When diluted by the average runoff from snow and rain, these 300 pounds would annually add an average salt concentration of 20 parts per million to the nation's waters, an amount comparable to the total dissolved salts in a clear mountain stream. Industrial use of water for cleaning, processing, cooling, and municipal use (mainly sewage), coupled with the return flows of irrigation waters containing mineral salts picked up as the water percolates through the ground, have produced measurable increases in the total salt content of rivers such as the industrial Ohio and the agricultural Colorado. As a result of man's activities, since 1914 the total salt content of the Ohio River has increased by about 50 percent and that of the Colorado River by nearly 100 percent. Using projections of future population figures and economic activity, and assuming that present trends in consumption and technology will continue, we can predict that the average total concentration of salts in U.S. rivers could rise to 400 parts per million by the end of this century. Such water would have a definite salty taste, and the concentration would approach the upper limit recommended for human consumption, that is, 500 parts per million.

underground salinization

Near the coasts, salt can enter the fresh groundwater supply by a different route. Porous rocks such as sandstone and limestone, which lie beneath the land surface and extend seaward, act as underground channels for the flow of fresh water seaward or the migration of salt water landward. Under natural conditions, sea water is held back by the flow of fresh water that is continually replenished by precipitation. But when fresh water is pumped from wells along the coast, sea water may replace the fresh water in the underground porous rock formation (Figure 1-4). Eventually, the water pumped from the wells that tap these groundwater reservoirs deteriorates in quality as more and more sea water mixes with the fresh water. To prevent such encroachment of sea water the conditions of pumping and the locations of wells must be rigorously controlled. For many areas, such as Long Island, the New Jersey coast, Florida, and southern California, salt water encroachment already poses critical water management problems.

Potable fresh groundwater can be contaminated by deeper sources of saline groundwater. In general, the salinity of groundwater increases with depth, and below certain depths, which vary from place to place, the groundwater is too salty for most domestic uses. For instance, in the Chicago area, potable water occurs in various geologic formations to depths of about 1800 feet (about 550 meters), but in deeper rocks the water varies from brackish to quite saline. In most of the southern two-thirds of Illinois, potable water

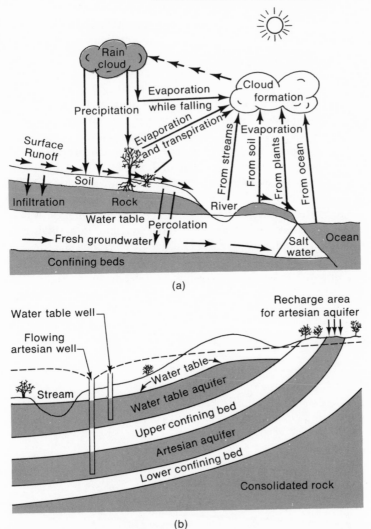

Figure 1-4. (a) Fresh groundwater layer below the earth's surface, fed by infiltrating and percolating water from precipitation. The groundwater table appears as a spring or river at the earth's surface. Note the boundary between fresh and salt water near ocean. (b) Two water-bearing rock strata (aquifers) separated by strata with little or no water. The artesian well flows freely because the level of the well lies below the water table level in the artesian aquifer (shown by the dotted line). SOURCE: *Groundwater and Wells* (Universal Oil Products Co., © 1966).

extends downward only to approximately 300 feet (about 91 meters), and below this depth the water is highly saline. The shallower potable water may become contaminated if this deep, mineralized water migrates upward as a result of excessive local pumping.

A more direct kind of salt pollution is now occurring in many areas of the northern United States where shallow groundwater has been contaminated by salt used for ice removal on streets and highways. In Connecticut and Massachusetts, along many of the principal highways up to 20 metric tons of salt are used every winter for each mile of road. The high solubility of sodium chloride, the salt most commonly used in ice removal, allows it to be washed easily into the ground and, from there, eventually into the groundwater below. In Illinois, salt water contamination was recently discovered when an ice-making machine in a small rural restaurant could no longer freeze water taken from a shallow well. The reason for the water's high salt content was traced to a nearby pile of salt left by the county highway department (Figure 1-5).

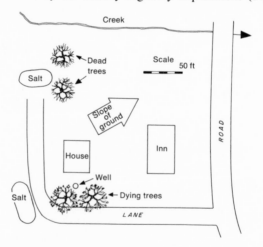

Figure 1-5. Contamination of groundwater and poisoning of trees resulting from storage of highway salt in Illinois. Water from a 27-foot (8.1-meter) well serving a house and inn was discovered to have a high salt content when the ice machine at the inn would not freeze the water. Highway salt had been stored along the lane for two years previously, was dissolved and carried by rainfall down to the water table about 7 feet (roughly 2 meters) below ground surface, and then moved laterally through the groundwater reservoir to the well. (Data from James P. Gibb, Illinois State Water Survey.)

As these examples indicate, dissolved salt can be an insidious and ubiquitous contaminant of our water supplies. Nearly every human activity tends to increase the concentration of salt in our surface and underground water reservoirs. The accumulation of salt will inevitably continue and increase over the coming decades, and there is no inexpensive way of removing salt from water. Fresh water has thus become another one of our dwindling national resources.

COPPER: THE PRICE OF COMFORT AND CONVENIENCE

Consumption of copper, among all the industrial metals, is perhaps the most indicative of the living standard and luxuries enjoyed by a nation. Without copper, such electronic and mechanical marvels as jet airliners, electronic computers, and television, typical of the so-called developed countries, would not be feasible. And compared with the rest of the world, the United States is the largest producer and consumer of copper (Figure 1-6).

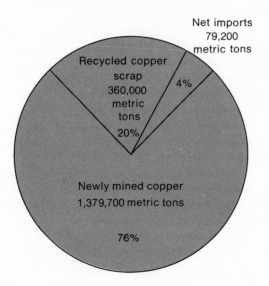

Figure 1-6. Sources of the 1,817,900 metric tons of copper used in the United States in 1971.

To understand the technical problems, cost, and environmental impact involved in producing so much copper, we have to consider the steps leading to the production of a single ton of pure copper. This process begins with exploring for the ore, followed by developing the ore body, mining and milling to extract and concentrate the ore minerals, and, finally, smelting and refining.

Exploration includes geologic field studies, measurements with geophysical instruments, exploratory drilling, and the assaying of samples. Major mining companies in the United States spend more than $100 million each year in search of new ore deposits; of this amount, about one-third is spent looking for copper ore.

Let's assume that an ore body similar to the many large, low-grade deposits of the southwestern United States has been found, and that it is suitable for open pit mining, the standard technique for extracting such deposits. The average mine today contains about 0.6 percent recoverable copper. About 362 metric tons of waste rock and 151.5 metric tons of ore will have to be removed for each ton of copper extracted, thereby leaving a hole in the ground as big as a small house (7400 cubic feet) and an equivalent pile of waste rock on the ground nearby.

The 151.5 metric tons of ore-bearing rock taken from the mine are brought to a mill where they are finely ground to separate the metallic minerals from the worthless matrix, or gangue. This process will produce almost 3 metric tons of concentrate and 145.5 metric tons (2800 cubic feet) of finely ground rock, or tailings, which must be deposited in settling ponds to prevent silting in natural waterways. The mill operation requires 90,000 gallons (341,000 liters) of water, up to two-thirds of which is recycled, and 3340 kilowatt-hours of electricity, equivalent to almost half a metric ton of coal.

The concentrate, consisting primarily of copper and iron sulfide minerals, now goes to the smelter where it is mixed with limestone and quartz sand. The smelting process is complicated, but essentially it burns off the sulfur in the concentrate, removes the iron as a glassy slag, and produces molten, impure "blister copper." With each metric ton of copper thus resulting, approximately 1.8 metric tons of slag are produced, and 0.9 metric ton of sulfur is burned, which yields 1.8 metric tons of sulfur dioxide gas. Part of the sulfur

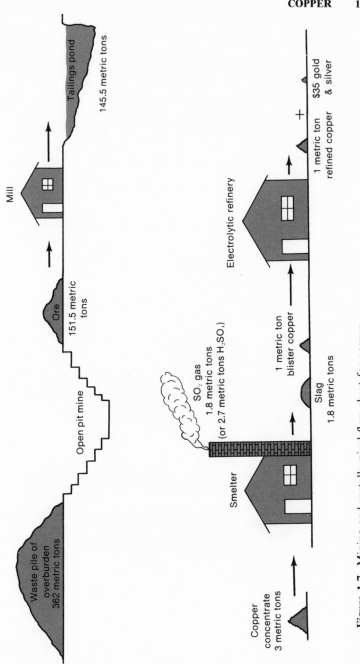

Figure 1-7. Mining and metallurgical flow sheet for copper.

dioxide may be converted to sulfuric acid; usually 2.7 metric tons of acid are produced for every 1.8 metric tons of sulfur dioxide gas, but some of the gas is vented into the atmosphere. In smelting this metric ton of copper concentrate, about 22 million BTU's (5544 $\times$ 10^6 calories) of heat are consumed, an amount equivalent to 22,000 cubic feet (622 $\times$ 10^6 cubic meters) of natural gas or almost 1 metric ton of soft coal.

Further treatment of the 1 metric ton of blister copper in an electrolytic refinery yields pure copper and about $35 worth of gold and silver as a by-product. This last process requires roughly 1250 kilowatt-hours of electricity. Figure 1-7 illustrates the mining and metallurgical steps necessary to produce pure copper from its ore.

Most uses of copper are related to the metal's high conductivity of heat and electricity, together with its malleability and ease of working. Copper alloys, chiefly brass and bronze, also have a variety of important uses. Nearly all of this metric ton of copper will be converted to wire, water piping, and tubing. The principal uses of copper in the United States are shown in Figure 1-8.

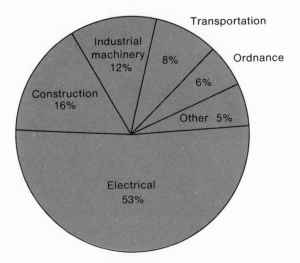

Figure 1-8. Principal uses of copper by industry in the United States in 1970.

The production of other industrial metals has similar environmental impact in terms of rock removal from the mine, waste rock piled somewhere nearby, and tailings impounded; large quantities of water and energy are also required. The slag and stack gases from the refining process must be disposed of in some way, and finally, when the mine is exhausted, an ugly landscape of gaping holes, piles of bare rock, decaying buildings, and rusting machinery is all that remains.

Although we are all ready to admit that the environmental impact of mining and refining operations is mostly detrimental, we do not always see the implications of reducing such impact or avoiding it altogether. Either we do without the goods provided by mining and metallurgical technology, or we pay more for those goods to meet the expense of limiting pollution and to leave the area in an acceptable condition before abandoning the mine, mill, and smelter.

NATURAL GEOLOGIC HAZARDS

Hardly a day passes without news of a great natural disaster somewhere in the world: earthquake, flood, volcanic eruption, hurricane, tsunami, or landslide. Such events are often referred to as "acts of God," as though some capricious deity were flailing away at mankind. But people are victims of such disasters usually because they have placed themselves directly in the path of some natural geologic process which then becomes a "hazard." We can seldom avoid being subjected to these various natural forces, but more often than not we can avoid the worst effects if we are aware of their potential occurrence.

earthquakes

In many parts of California, earthquakes are fairly common. Residents of the state are aware of this hazard, and many even know the location of the very faults along which the earth moves. Fewer people, however, realize that under the influence of an earthquake, unconsolidated silts, sands, and muds may be exceedingly unstable. An earthquake of even moderate magnitude can destroy buildings constructed on such materials, while far less damage will be experienced in areas built on solid bedrock. Local governments have begun to establish zoning and building regulations to ensure that information about ground stability is available not only to builders but also to those buying houses in areas prone to earthquake damage.

The problem becomes more difficult when the frequency of occurrence of a major geologic force, like an earthquake, is not known, and previous occurrences are remote in time. For example, in 1811–1812, the southeastern corner of Missouri was severely shaken by a series of tremors that produced damage over a far greater area than the typical major California earthquake. Yet the central United States is not currently considered an active seismic region because it has had no destructive earthquakes in more recent times. The possibility of new earthquakes in this region certainly exists, but it is almost impossible to say just when they might happen. What importance should we give to our knowledge that such major earthquakes could come at any time? How much are we willing to spend to earthquake-proof houses, schools, hospitals, gas lines, bridges, and other structures against such a poorly defined risk? And yet we know the risk is real and potentially devastating to human life and property.

floods

From earliest recorded human history to the present day, floods from rivers and the sea have been regarded as inevitable. Although high waters might be inevitable, the damage and loss of life they cause certainly need not be. The coastal areas and lands adjacent to a river's edge must be considered as part of the marine or fluvial environment; for these marginal areas are, by their very nature, always subject to periodic flooding, if only fleetingly. Because of this occasional, intermittent occupancy of coastal and fluvial land by water, humans must be prepared to "share" these lands with the sea and the rivers. This is actually the case when we use seashores and valleys for recreation. It certainly is not the case when we settle permanently in such areas, because our housing, commercial, and industrial facilities always will be subject to flooding, even though the risk of occupancy is judged low compared with the assumed value of these lands. In this regard, consider the Rapid City flood in South Dakota (1972), where the only "blame" was placed on the local residents' failure to take action when warned of the impending high water and dam collapse.

Land-use planning involves evaluation of risks from natural phenomena. However dispersed in time and space, volcanic eruptions, landslides, flash floods, earthquakes, tsunami, tornados, and hurricanes are all natural forces of immense magnitude. Whether or not their impact on human society is significant depends on our decisions about land-use, building style, and population distribution. We need to consider that human values are at stake when exploiting areas potentially endangered by these geologic forces, how important such values are, and what steps can be taken to assure their most intelligent realization.

The various problems posed in this chapter—whether problems of energy supply, waste disposal, trace elements, salinization of surface and ground waters, depletion of copper, or geologic hazards—demonstrate the inherent difficulties of using our natural resources to support the good life because of the accompanying costs of using, degrading, and depleting those resources. This situation jeopardizes not only our own future tenancy on this planet but that of generations to come.

2

the earth
in space and time

If we want to survive on this planet, let alone live in harmony with it, we must take an inventory of our present and future needs to evaluate intelligently how to conserve and manage its resources and environments for our own and succeeding generations. And this evaluation can be fully effective only if made within the appropriate perspective. This chapter, therefore, presents some of the more important geologic concepts and principles that bear on current and anticipated environmental questions and problems. We discuss the long history of the earth and the many slow but inexorable changes it has experienced; the natural equilibrium between the earth's form and the processes modifying that form; the natural cycles of change and renewal that keep the earth in constant flux and motion; and finally the evolution of life, ever adapting to the changing earth, with man's recent appearance and his growing impact as an agent of change.

EARTH HISTORY

One of geology's most significant contributions to human thought is the recognition of the extreme antiquity of the earth. As interest in the natural world increased during the eighteenth and nineteenth centuries, men slowly developed an historical perspective toward nature. Today we realize that to understand the world of nature—whether landscapes, the oceans, floras and faunas, or man himself—we must view the present as the historical product of a constantly changing past that reaches far back in time. Even after the ecclesiastical edict establishing 4004 B.C. as the earth's creation date was discounted by geologic evidence (leading early in our century to estimates of 40 to 50 million years), it was not until the development and refinement of "radioactive clocks" in the past 25 to 30 years that we discovered the great age of the earth: 4.5 billion years. Thus, modern man has had relatively little time to adjust his thinking to the significance of this greatly lengthened perspective.

geologic time

As an historical science, geology has established a chronology for the earth's past history that gives some basis for projections into the future. Geology similarly provides a dynamic evolutionary explanation of how historical events and phenomena were related to and dependent on each other (Figures 2-1 and 2-2). For example, geologic chronology indicates that 300 to 500 million years ago, the land areas of the world were encompassed in one or two supercontinents. During the last 200 million years, however, these great land masses have slowly separated into the present continents. This dynamic, evolutionary view of earth history explains the chronology of changing continental shape as a result of the relative movement of crustal plates, carrying the continental fragments with them as they move in different directions.

Study of rocks exposed in the earth's crust, of meteorites, and, most recently, of lunar samples returned by Apollo space missions reveals that the earth is about 4.5 billion years old. For approximately its first billion years the earth was completely lifeless. According to one theory, during this time the planet, which was

ERA	PERIOD	EPOCH	MAJOR EVENTS IN EARTH HISTORY
CENOZOIC	Quaternary	Holocene —10,000— Pleistocene —2,500,000—	Earliest man — Modern horse evolves in North America, then dies out — Ice Ages — Grand Canyon carved — Cascade Range and Pacific Coast Ranges formed
CENOZOIC	Tertiary	Pliocene —7,000,000— Miocene —26,000,000— Oligocene —38,000,000— Eocene —54,000,000— Paleocene —65,000,000—	Rapid spread and evolution of grazing mammals; Earliest elephants; First primitive horses, rhinoceroses, and camels; First primates
MESOZOIC	Cretaceous —136,000,000—		Extinction of dinosaurs; Great evolution and spread of flowering plants; Half of North America covered by seas; Initial uplift and folding of Rocky Mountains; Initial uplift of Sierra Nevada
MESOZOIC	Jurassic —190,000,000—		First birds and mammals; Dinosaurs at their peak — Dinosaurs
MESOZOIC	Triassic —225,000,000—		Arid climates in much of western North America
PALEOZOIC	Permian —280,000,000—		Mammal-like reptiles; Ice Ages in Southern Hemisphere; World climate much like today; Deserts in western United States
PALEOZOIC	Pennsylvanian —325,000,000—		First reptiles — Large insects; Widespread swamps, coal source; Tropical climate in United States; Uplift and folding of Appalachian Mountains
PALEOZOIC	Mississippian —345,000,000—		Widespread flooding of North America, limestone deposited; Sharks abundant
PALEOZOIC	Devonian —395,000,000—		First amphibians; First forests — Trilobites
PALEOZOIC	Silurian —430,000,000—		First air-breathing animals (scorpions) First land plants; Deserts in eastern and central U.S.
PALEOZOIC	Ordovician —500,000,000—		Trilobites at peak; First vertebrates (fish); Widespread flooding of North America by seas
PALEOZOIC	Cambrian —570,000,000—		Marine shelled invertebrates common; First abundant animal fossils
PRECAMBRIAN	PROTEROZOIC —2,500,000,000—		Marine invertebrates probably common; few with shells (1,200,000,000); Glaciation—probably worldwide; Many mountain systems uplifted and eroded
PRECAMBRIAN	ARCHEOZOIC —4,500,000,000—		Earliest plants (3,200,000,000)

Figure 2-1. Geologic time scale showing major time divisions and important events in the history of the earth and of life. SOURCE: *Investigating the Earth,* Earth Science Curriculum Project (Houghton Mifflin Co., Boston, 1967), p. 425.

created by the gravitational accretion of many small "planetesi-mal" particles, slowly heated up, initially from the energy released

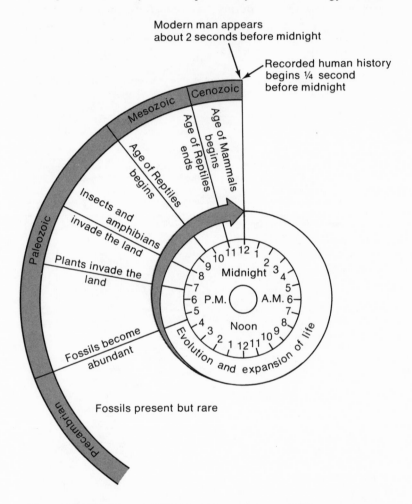

Figure 2-2. The history of life on a 24-hour scale, starting some two billion years ago with the appearance of primitive photosynthetic plants. Shown this way, we see how initially slow the evolution and expansion of life was, how recently mammals and man have appeared, and how little time, proportionately, human history represents. SOURCE: Simpson and Beck, *Life: An Introduction to Biology* (Harcourt, Brace, and Jovanovich, New York, 1965).

by compaction and from the radioactive decay of certain elements. This heating caused the earth to melt partially so that it slowly differentiated into a layered body with a large iron–nickel core, surrounded by a thick mantle of iron–magnesium silicates, and covered with a thin crust of aluminum-rich silicate minerals (Figure 2-3). The earth's initial atmosphere and hydrosphere were formed by the volcanic release of gases from the earth's interior to the exterior. These gases were mainly water vapor, which condensed into liquid water and produced the primeval seas. Other gases were methane, ammonia, carbon dioxide, and probably some carbon monoxide, all of which existed in the early atmosphere.

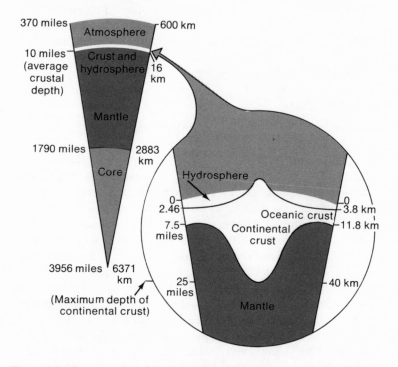

Figure 2-3. Cross section of earth showing differentiation into core (iron–nickel), mantle (iron–magnesium silicates), crust (aluminum–iron silicates), hydrosphere (water), and atmosphere (nitrogen–oxygen). Note that the crust is several times thicker under the continents than under the oceans. SOURCE: B. Skinner, *Earth Resources* (Prentice-Hall, Inc., Englewood Cliffs, N.J., 1969), p. 17.

changing landscapes

Since then the earth has not remained static: Mountains have been slowly raised and gradually eroded by water and wind; rivers have traced their courses across the lands, carrying sediment to the sea; lava has poured over the earth's surface; and portions of the continents have subsided below the sea only to be raised again. And so for billions of years the earth has undergone many changes, experienced many cycles of erosion and sediment deposition, mountain building, and climatic variations, and has nurtured many millions of generations of slowly evolving life.

Because of our own relatively short life span, we tend to see the earth as essentially fixed and unchanging. Those processes of natural change that we do recognize are, from our perspective, so slow that they seem inconsequential. But given the great age of the earth, these processes have resulted in many new landscapes appearing and disappearing throughout the long flow of earth history.

enter humans

When looking at our interaction with the natural world, it is important to appreciate this long and eventful history of the earth. Consider, for example, the role of food in supporting all our human activities. Green plants make food by photosynthesis, thereby converting radiant solar energy into stored chemical energy. Some of this energy is passed on to animals that feed on green plants; and these plant eaters (herbivores), in turn, supply energy to the meat eaters (carnivores) that feed upon them. Thus, whether we eat breakfast cereal, honey, or steak, the energy from our food comes ultimately from the sun and the plant life it supports.

The soils in which plants grow are the result of complex geologic and biologic processes, usually acting over long periods of time. Soils are developed from the weathering of either the underlying rocks of the earth's crust or, more commonly, the surface layers laid down by streams and rivers, winds and glaciers, and lakes. Soil-building vegetation and soil organisms including bacteria, fungi, worms, and insects contribute at least as much to soil formation as do the physical and chemical processes of weathering. Although soils form at different rates, most highly fertile soils take hundreds or thousands of years to develop. And even though natural erosion alone will remove soil, agriculture increases the rate of soil erosion 10 to 100 times or more. The significance of soils in human affairs is treated more thoroughly later.

As another example of time's importance in developing resources useful to humans, we can consider how long it takes to form coal. Minable coal seams, usually less than a few meters thick, represent thousands of years of plant accumulation, followed by millions of years of burial and compression within the earth's crust to remove excess water and volatile substances and to produce a dense, carbon-rich product. Once mined and burned, coals are forever lost and the world's supply of energy thereby diminished. There are present-day coal-forming environments, such as the Florida Everglades, but it is unreasonable to suppose that these potential coals will be available for man's use in the foreseeable future.

The present natural condition of the earth is, as we have noted, the result of geologic and biologic processes operating over many eons. Therefore, to understand the full implications of the earth's present condition, we must have some notion of the processes that brought it to that condition.

EARTH PROCESSES

We know that the history of the earth is one of constant change. What are some of the major geologic processes responsible for this change? How do they bear on our contemporary environmental concerns?

erosion and sedimentation

Rocks exposed at the earth's surface are continuously subject to weathering and erosion that slowly cause them to disintegrate and dissolve, and to be moved and deposited elsewhere. The dissolving action of rainfall causes the initial weathering of rocks by removing small but measurable amounts of their chemical constituents. Rain will also wash away particles of rock that have been loosened by the freezing action of winter ice, or by the rootlets of summer vegetation. As water from rainfall flows along the ground surface, it picks up these small rock grains and transports them first in tiny rivulets, then in streams and rivers. Billions of tons of dissolved substances and suspended sediments are thus transported by runoff from upland areas to the continental margins, farther downslope. There the sediments may be temporarily deposited, although with time they will be washed up and down the coasts by longshore currents or carried farther out to sea, first across the continental shelves, then into the ocean deeps. Every year the Mississippi River alone carries about 450 million metric tons of eroded material (roughly half a cubic mile or 2.08 cubic kilometers) from the continental United States to the Gulf of Mexico.

Not all sediment that has been weathered and eroded at the earth's surface is carried by water. Wind, blowing across the land surface, picks up the finer particles and eventually deposits them at sea, where they may remain in suspension for a while, and eventually settle to the ocean floor. Ice, too, during those occasional times when parts of the earth go through a glacial period, flows under its own accumulated weight and moves rock and sediment slowly downslope. These materials also ultimately find their way to the seas.

Not all materials eroded from continents are deposited on the ocean floor as sedimentary particles. Some materials carried by streams and rivers are dissolved substances that remain in solution in sea water. For example, the Mississippi River, in addition to its load of suspended sediment (303 million metric tons), each year carries 125 million metric tons of dissolved salts to the Gulf of Mexico. The saltiness of sea water is due to many millions of years of accumulation of these highly soluble substances in the oceans.

Thus, from land erosion there is a net transport of sediments from the continents to the ocean basins, even though there may be temporary deposition in river valleys, lakes, marshes, or interior sedimentary basins. Present erosion rates, if continued without uplift of the land, would wear the continents to sea level in about 50 million years.

enter pollutants

The processes of erosion and sedimentation provide a perspective from which we can view some of our current environmental problems. In the weathering and erosion of land and in the transportation and deposition of its sediment, not only are natural materials carried in streams and rivers to lakes and oceans, but virtually all of man's wastes on the earth's surface enter these cycles. For example, pesticides and herbicides are brought by surface runoff and atmospheric precipitation into the oceans, where they accumulate in the water and in marine organisms living in the sea.

DDT residues.   In the 25 years that DDT has been employed on land, its residues have been slowly entering the world's oceans, where the present concentration is estimated at one part per trillion. Even though this concentration may seem negligible, some organisms take up DDT residues in their tissues disproportionately, and the concentration increases upward in the food chain. For example, predatory seabirds feed on fish that feed, in turn, on microscopic animals and plants floating in the sea. These birds contain roughly 10 parts per million DDT; this represents a 10 millionfold increase in concentration. At these concentrations, DDT residues interfere with the biochemistry of eggshell formation, and now many species of birds, such as the brown pelican of California, are apparently facing extinction. Thus, however local initial applications of DDT may be, various natural processes will inevitably take small amounts of this chemical far beyond the place where it originated. Gradually, these small amounts will build up in concentration, often reaching toxic levels in living organisms. Although DDT has been important in controlling disease-carrying insects like the malarial mosquito, and crop-destroying pests like aphids, the long-term effects of DDT are somewhat doubtful. It is contaminating the biosphere, and strains of pests have developed a resistance to DDT; therefore, either stronger doses or new pesticides are required for their control, which further compounds the problem. The Environmental Protection Agency, with its virtual ban of DDT, has recognized the seriousness of this problem.

Carbon dioxide and sulfur dioxide.   Another example of how natural processes become involved with pollution is the way weathering effects are aggravated by air pollutants. In humid climates, water in the air has small amounts of carbon dioxide dissolved in it, thus making it slightly acidic. When it falls as rain, this weakly acidic water will dissolve surface rocks, especially marble and limestone. In areas where industrial plants have belched large quantities of sulfur dioxide into the air—as well as increased the natural levels of carbon dioxide—solution is enhanced still further because the rain combines with the sulfur dioxide and makes highly corrosive sulfuric acid. Cleopatra's Needle, a granite obelisk brought from Egypt to New York City's Central Park in the late nineteenth century, is a classic example of such weathering. For almost 3400 years, in the clean, dry air of Egypt, this monument retained its elaborate hieroglyphic surface carvings, but in the last half century, two of its carved faces (those on the south and west sides facing the prevailing winds) have been completely obliterated; the other two faces, away from the prevailing winds, are less heavily weathered.

In Venice, Italy, similar rapid weathering of buildings and statues, many of them made of marble, has seriously defaced that city's beautiful monuments. Virtually all this weathering has occurred in the last 50 years. Photographs of these same structures taken at the turn of the century reveal almost no serious weathering effects although the structures had already been standing for several centuries. An increase in the acidity of rain also results in other problems such as the more intensive leaching of nutrients from soil (particularly phosphorus), and local fish kills, as in Sweden, where highly acidic rain enters fresh water lakes. Clearly, pollutants in the air have greatly accelerated some weathering processes and locally have had unfortunate side effects on some forms of life (Figure 2-4).

deformation of the earth's crust

The earth is an active body, as demonstrated by generally widespread tectonic movements such as the faulting and folding of rocks, earthquakes, and mountain building. The basic causes of the earth's tectonic activity are still uncertain. One cause may be, in part at least, the slow, fluid-like convective motion within the earth's mantle, which is the region lying above the core and below the surface rocks, or crust.

Plate tectonics.   Recent exploration of the world's oceans combined with past studies of the continents suggest that the earth's crust is composed of several large, relatively rigid plates that move independently of each other. The high submarine ridges lying in

Figure 2-4. Marble statue of The Temperance, Palazzo Ducale, Venice. The large increase in air pollutants in the past few decades has resulted in severe weathering. Perhaps the statue would now be better called "The Statue of Dissolution"! SOURCE: The Italian Art & Landscape Foundation, Inc. Photographer: G. Lotti.

the mid oceans mark one type of plate boundary; here the plates are slowly drifting apart, and new material is added to the plates in the form of basaltic lava. At other boundaries, one of the plates may slide under another and form a deep oceanic trench at the boundary. An example is the Peru Trench on the west side of South America. The plates may also slide horizontally past each other and make long vertical fracture zones, such as the San Andreas fault in California. From a human standpoint the motion of these plates is very slow, at most, 2 or 3 inches (5–8 centimeters) per year; however, over geologic time the movement may total thousands of miles. Although the plates seem to be moving continuously, the friction at their boundaries is great, and may periodically inhibit movement there. As the stresses accumulate, the friction is eventually overcome and the consequent spasmodic and rapid motion along the boundaries gives rise to earthquakes. These lateral and vertical movements at the boundaries of crustal plates account for much of the earthquake activity along the mid-ocean ridges and continental margins, particularly around the Pacific Ocean.

Plate tectonics, then, seem to account for much of the earth's present-day activity. By studying the earth's past, as recorded in the rocks in the earth's crust, we can see that plate movements have been occurring for several hundred million years, and perhaps even longer. The flooding of broad continental areas by ancient seas has also happened frequently in the past. In many instances it is still a moot question among geologists as to whether the continents have subsided or the seas have risen—or both! In either case, the transgression and subsequent regression of seas are probably the result of crustal activity related to plate tectonics.

Glaciation. At times in earth history glaciation has caused major changes in sea level. Sea levels are lowered several hundred feet during glaciation as large quantities of water are withdrawn from the sea to make continental ice sheets. Sea level is raised again as the ice melts during an interglacial warming such as the present. For example, during the last glacial epoch, sea level was approximately 450 feet (137 meters) lower than now; and if all the ice remaining in today's ice sheets were melted, sea level would rise about 200 feet (approximately 60 meters).

As we occupy more of the earth, building complex cities and civilizations, we should be aware of the earth's crustal movements. We know the horizontal dimensions and the boundary regions of the major plates, as well as their average rates of movement. Even though yearly rates of motion may be small and irregular along plate boundaries, we can expect some significant movement, often expressed as earthquakes, within every few decades. Multi-storied buildings, housing developments on filled land, nuclear reactors, dams, or water and gas mains—when built in tectonically active areas—may be victims of such movement, causing enormous casualties and damage. Rather than viewing earthquakes as freaks of nature, we must learn to expect them, and plan for them, as natural events, even though the *exact* time and place of each occurrence is as yet largely unpredictable.

state of equilibrium

Although the earth is continuously undergoing changes, the rates of change are often exceedingly slow. Indeed, some features of the landscape are in a kind of balance or equilibrium. Thus, many rivers flow within self-formed channels built by the river from sediments deposited in its channel and on its floodplain, as, for example, the Mississippi or the Nile. Both the cross section and the gradient, or slope, of the river are adjusted over a period of years to the flow of water and to the volume and characteristics of the sediment transported by the river. In a similar manner, the shape and size of a beach often represent a balance achieved as waves work and rework sand continuously supplied to, and removed from, the beach by streams and shoreline currents.

Along a river, works of man such as dams, canals, or diversions to straighten it, can seriously disturb the natural equilibrium. Unless restrained by dikes or other controls, a crooked river will return to being crooked after it is straightened. A dam creates a pool so that, upstream, sediment will be deposited in the artificial lake behind the dam, eventually filling it. The water flow just below the dam carries little or no sediment, so it is capable of eroding the riverbed downstream. The change in flow and the absence of silt result in erosion until the modified downstream flow has a sediment load appropriate to the new flow (Figure 2-5). If, however, tributaries below the dam contribute enough sediment, the reduced water

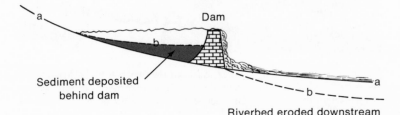

Figure 2-5. Hypothetical river seen in cross section before damming (a) and after (b). Sediment accumulates upstream in the reservoir created behind the dam and sediment is eroded downstream of the dam.

Figure 2-6. Aerial view, looking south, of the beach front in Miami with its many luxury hotels. When the hotels were originally built several decades ago, there were many feet of natural beach that have since been eroded by longshore currents. A sea wall roughly 10 feet (3 meters) high was subsequently built to prevent further erosion. Jetties were also constructed at right angles to the sea wall to accumulate some of the drifting sediment carried by the currents. In one area along the sea wall, sand has built up to the top of the wall. SOURCE: Florida Department of Natural Resources, Bureau of Beaches and Shores.

flow may not be able to remove the sediment. The river then becomes choked with sediment and may require dredging.

Along coasts, beaches may be starved for sand if rivers that supply the sand are dammed so the sand is trapped in reservoirs behind the dams. Human interference with the beach itself also can produce drastic changes (Figure 2-6). Breakwaters placed offshore to diminish the force of waves inshore often cause beaches to move seaward because the sediment brought to the beach, usually by longshore currents, no longer is being removed by wave action. Conversely, offshore dredging of sand and gravel can disturb the natural beach and inshore profile. Beach sediment inshore is eroded and deposited offshore to replace the material that has been removed and thus restore equilibrium. Inlets cutting through a beach and protected by long jetties may accumulate sand on one side where a longshore current is obstructed; whereas on the other side of the inlet the beach, now starved for sand, may begin to erode.

Many natural earth systems closely approach a condition of balance and maintain it over relatively long periods. Even where the land is slowly being eroded, hillslopes and rivers may continue to retain forms that change very little over time. These equilibrium forms or settings provide the dynamic but consistent environments for living things. In the time scale of human activity, evolutionary changes of these physical environments may be exceedingly slow. Rapid changes of the environment, however, will alter the natural balance achieved by processes acting over long periods of time.

THE EARTH AS A CLOSED SYSTEM

In our short life span we do not easily recognize the continuing geologic changes that the earth's surface experiences. Most of these processes work at such slow rates that, except for the occasional earthquake, volcanic eruption, or flood, we see the earth as virtually static and immutable. Moreover, because we humans are dwarfed by the scale of most of the earth's features—mountains, oceans, plains and plateaus, forests, and deserts—we tend to think of our planet as an infinite reservoir for our resources and our wastes. Just as there once seemed to be no end to the earth's bounty in soils, minerals, and fuels, there also seemed to be no limit to the area available for our domestic and industrial wastes. But of course the earth does have limits.

The processes acting on the earth are mostly cyclical rather than "one way." The water that falls today as rain will eventually reach the sea, where it will be evaporated and return to the atmosphere, and from there fall once again. These cycles may take from a few years to several millions of years to reach completion. Not all earth processes operate in regular, periodic cycles; rather, there are many natural fluctuations, and their rhythms are important to humans.

natural cycles

From the physical principle of the conservation of mass, we know that matter, however it may be altered physically or chemically, is always conserved. The fuel we burn may seem to disappear, but actually it is converted to gases, solid ash, and heat. So, too, with the earth. Although its materials may be changed physically and chemically, or moved from place to place, the solid earth–water–air system remains one closed cycle. In this section we describe two natural cycles, the rock cycle and the water cycle. These cycles illustrate how the earth is truly a closed system, in that material is constantly recycled and conserved, however many changes it may experience in the process.

Rock cycles. In the rock cycle, molten rock, or magma, from the upper part of the earth's mantle crystallizes as igneous rock such as granite or basalt (Figure 2-7). Weathering and erosion of these igneous rocks yield sediments that after burial, compaction, and cementation become sedimentary rocks such as sandstone, shale, and limestone. Buried with the sediments may be the skeletal remains of animals or plants. Sedimentary rocks (as well as other types) exposed to high pressures and temperatures will be changed or "metamorphosed" into new or metamorphic rocks such as slates, schists, marbles, and gneisses. If a thick accumulation of sedimentary rocks is remelted as a result of deep burial within the crust or incorporation within the mantle, it will form new magma. Such magma eventually will cool and solidify to "new" igneous rock, thus initiating a new cycle. Sedimentary and metamorphic rocks are, of course, also subject to weathering and erosion, which results in "second-stage" sediments.

It can be a valuable exercise to consider a grain of quartz on a sandy beach and to speculate on how many, how lengthy, and what kinds of cycles it's been through: from igneous rock to sediment to schist to magma to igneous rock to sediment again. Such specula-

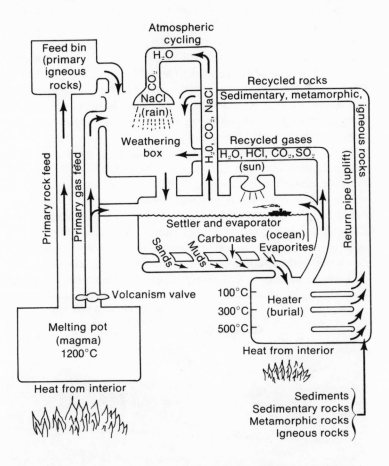

Figure 2-7. The rock cycle shown schematically. The cycle is driven in part from the heat resulting from the decay of naturally occurring radioactive isotopes, principally uranium, thorium, and potassium, in the earth's crust. Solar energy drives the hydrologic cycle that results in erosion and sedimentation at the earth's surface. SOURCE: R. M. Garrels and F. T. Mackenzie, *Evolution of Sedimentary Rocks* (W. W. Norton & Co., Inc., New York, 1971), p. 330.

tion is not merely of academic interest, for we must have some insight into the timing and mechanics of cycles within the earth if we want to avoid making unreasonable or impossible demands on it. For example, a recent suggestion for solid-waste disposal involves the dumping of wastes into deep-sea trenches. Sedimentation within the trench would bury the waste, and eventually the waste material would be incorporated within the base of the continent (Figure 2-8). Although this waste-disposal technique was somewhat facetiously suggested to solve the growing problem of solid-waste disposal, it may actually be a practicable solution. Before such disposal is undertaken, we must have more accurate knowledge of the sedimentation rate and the dynamics of this major earth cycle of plate tectonics.

Many substances useful to man occur in various parts of the rock cycle as either dispersed, concentrated, or simply "available." For example, phosphate is dispersed as PO_4^{3-} ions in the sea water and as the calcium-phosphate mineral, apatite, in granite; as certain ore-bearing beds in the Phosphoria Formation of Wyoming and Colorado, in bone, and as animal manure, it is concentrated; and as soluble phosphates in soil, it is available. Many industrial activities begin with a substance in its concentrated or available form and, after a number of processes, disperse it. And, once dispersed,

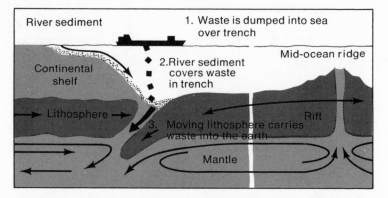

Figure 2-8. Schematic diagram illustrating how solid wastes could be disposed of in a deep-sea trench. Waste is covered by land-derived sediment and eventually carried beneath continent by the sea floor which plunges below it.

many substances no longer can be concentrated or made available again.

Water cycle.   In the water cycle, every year large quantities of water evaporate from the oceans, most returning to the oceans as snow or rain (Figure 2-9). About 10 percent, however, joins the moisture that evaporates over the lands and falls on the land. Almost two-thirds of the precipitation on the land is reevaporated; the more than one-third remaining returns to the sea as runoff from the land.

Only a fraction of the total hydrosphere is cycled each year. Large quantities of water are stored in the oceans, in fresh water

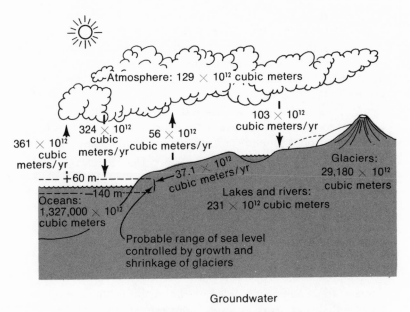

Figure 2-9. The hydrosphere and the exchange of water among its different parts during the year. SOURCE: B. Skinner, *Earth Resources* (Prentice-Hall, Inc., Englewood Cliffs, N.J., 1969), p. 131.

lakes and rivers, in glacial snow and ice, as subsurface groundwater, and, of course, in living animals and plants. Eventually, though, all this water will reenter the cycle.

As the rock and water cycles demonstrate, materials on the earth do not simply disappear even though they move from place to place. This concept is important when, for example, we wish to dispose of wastes. It is not enough to know that wastes will be diluted or dispersed from their place of origin; we must also know where they are likely to go, how soon, and in what concentrations, and how long they will stay there.

rates and residence time

Recognizing that the earth is a closed system (or, perhaps more accurately, a combination of many closed systems), and that materials are continually cycled and recycled, we ought to know how fast these processes occur. For example, if we wish to dispose of highly radioactive wastes from a nuclear power plant, we need to know whether the natural recycling of the wastes will be sufficiently slow so that they will have decayed to a radioactive level harmless to life by the time they "reappear." Or, if water is to be withdrawn from a groundwater reservoir, we should know the rate of recharge so that removal of water can be regulated accordingly. Hence, we must know not only the nature of a given cycle, but also the rate at which it proceeds, and the length of time materials reside within different parts of the cycle. Tables 2-1 and 2-2 present a variety of typical rates and residence times for several different natural cycles.

nonrenewable and renewable resources

Some of the materials provided by the earth for human use have taken millions of years to form. Their rate of consumption is so much faster than their rate of formation that the materials must be considered as nonrenewable resources. Thus, for all practical human purposes, the amounts of oil, gas, and coal, as well as some of the major industrial metals like copper, lead, and zinc, are fixed and finite. Obviously, the faster we consume these nonrenewable resources, the more rapidly the total supply diminishes. However, with some metals we can at times follow nature's example and recycle and reuse discarded metallic products. Such recycling, which is difficult and expensive for metals, is impossible for fossil fuels.

Other earth materials, such as food crops, livestock, forest products (lumber and wood pulp), and natural fibers (wool and cotton),

TABLE 2-1. RESIDENCE TIMES OF SOME NATURAL CYCLES

Earth Materials	Some Typical Residence Times
Atmosphere circulation	
Water vapor	10 days (lower atmosphere)
Carbon dioxide	5 to 10 days (with sea)
Aerosol particles	
Stratosphere (upper atmosphere)	Several months to several years
Troposphere (lower atmosphere)	One to several weeks
Hydrosphere circulation	
Atlantic surface water	10 years
Atlantic deep water	600 years
Pacific surface water	25 years
Pacific deep water	1300 years
Terrestrial groundwater	150 years [above 2500 feet (760 meters) depth]
Biosphere circulation[a]	
Water	2,000,000 years
Oxygen	2000 years
Carbon dioxide	300 years
Sea water constituents[a]	
Water	44,000 years
All salts	22,000,000 years
Calcium ion	1,200,000 years
Sulfate ion	11,000,000 years
Sodium ion	260,000,000 years
Chloride ion	Infinite

[a]Average time it takes for these materials to recycle with the atmosphere and hydrosphere.

TABLE 2-2. RATES OF SOME NATURAL CYCLES

Earth Processes	Some Typical Rates
Erosion	
Average U.S. erosion rate[a]	2.4 inches (6.1 cm) per thousand years
Colorado River drainage area	6.5 inches (16.5 cm) per thousand years
Mississippi River drainage area	2.0 inches (5.1 cm) per thousand years
N. Atlantic drainage area	1.9 inches (4.8 cm) per thousand years
Pacific slope (Calif.)	3.6 inches (9.1 cm) per thousand years
Sedimentation[b]	
Colorado River	281 million metric tons per year
Mississippi River	431 million metric tons per year
N. Atlantic Coast of U.S.	48 million metric tons per year
Pacific slope (Calif.)	76 million metric tons per year
Tectonism	
Sea floor spreading	
N. Atlantic	1 inch (2.5 cm) per year
East Pacific	3-4 inches (7-10 cm) per year
Faulting	
San Andreas (Calif.)	0.5 inch (1.3 cm) per year
Mountain uplift	
Cajon Pass, San Bernardino Mts., Calif	0.4 inch (1 cm) per year

[a]Thickness of the layer of surface of the continental United States eroded per 1000 years.

[b]Includes solid particles and dissolved salts.

are regenerated over and over, and so are considered renewable resources. Water is constantly and relatively rapidly being recycled by natural processes and, therefore, is also a renewable resource. But if man uses any of these resources faster than they can be naturally renewed, then they too will begin to diminish in quantity and quality as do nonrenewable resources.

Certain nonrenewable resources, such as aluminum, magnesium, and sulfur, are so abundant in the earth's crust or in sea water that, even though their concentration may be somewhat low, their supply will remain for many centuries. Their current exploitation is limited by the lack of relatively cheap energy to extract them from their sources, whether bulk rock or sea water. Some scientists believe that nuclear energy technology may ultimately provide a cheap source of extractive energy. But this forecast may be misleading because there are some materials that are of such low natural abundance in the earth's crust or in sea water that even this proposed energy source will not make their extraction economical. And the greatly increased use of nuclear energy that this practice would entail will create difficult environmental problems such as safe disposal of increased radioactive waste and increased thermal pollution of water and air. There also would be the problem of eliminating the enormous amount of rock waste resulting from the processing of bulk rock for its limited metal content.

EVOLUTION OF LIFE

Not only has the earth changed and evolved through time as a result of natural processes, but life on earth also has undergone numerous alterations. From the primitive atmosphere, rich in methane, ammonia, carbon dioxide, and water vapor, a variety of complex organic molecules formed in the sea. These molecules eventually led to the earliest life forms, about 3 billion years ago; these resembled living single-celled algae and bacteria. About this time, the crucial biologic process of plant photosynthesis evolved. In this process, carbon dioxide combines with water by using energy from the sun. The H_2 and CO_2 are converted into carbohydrate food, and oxygen is released. Through ever-increasing photosynthetic activity, and the separation of water vapor into molecules of hydrogen and oxygen by high energy radiation in the upper atmosphere, the earth's initial atmosphere was gradually modified. Subsequently, it was modified into one that is now mainly composed of nitrogen and oxygen with small amounts of carbon dioxide and traces of the noble gases (i.e., gases, such as helium and argon, that seldom combine with other elements). This atmospheric evolution probably took 2 or 3 billion years.

More than half a billion years ago, the first of the higher or more complex invertebrates appeared in the sea. These were followed some 150 million years later by primitive fish. As the oxygen content of the atmosphere increased over time, a layer of ozone (three atoms of oxygen bound together) formed in its upper regions. This ozone layer blocks out harmful ultraviolet radiation from the sun. In the sea such radiation penetrates only a few meters; hence, it did not affect life in the early oceans. But until the ozone layer had developed, life was restricted to water.

About 400 million years ago, the protective ozone layer developed sufficiently for life to invade dry land. The first invaders were plants and insects, soon followed by amphibians, and from them arose reptiles. About 200 million years after life developed on land, mammals appeared, gradually developing into many diverse types such as shrews, bats, whales, horses, lions, rabbits, and monkeys. About 2 million years ago, or one-twentieth of 1 percent of all earth history, man's African ancestors, the proto-human *australopithecines,* appeared.

environment and adaptation

Animals and plants depend on their surroundings for meeting their basic life needs of food, living space, and mates. Because the genetic background of each individual within a species is not identical, some members of the species will be more successful in surviving and rearing offspring than others. Through time, this differential reproductive success results in a gradual shift in the overall genetic composition of the species toward increasing adaptation to the environment. The species eventually optimizes its total genetic complex with respect to the environment. So long as the environment remains the same, the species retains its favorable adaptive position.

Much of the diversity and richness seen in the unfolding history of life reflects the spread of organisms from marine environments, where life presumably originated, to terrestrial environments. And within terrestrial environments there has been further expansion of life: from swampy coastal lowlands to interior plains and mountains; from forests to deserts; from a ground-dwelling way of life to life in the air and in the trees.

Life has thus undergone a tremendous expansion by colonizing the wide range of physical environments on the earth. Secondary opportunities for life appeared during this primary expansion as some forms evolved. For example, the evolutionary appearance of the grasses, which covered the semiarid plains and plateaus of the world, opened a new way of life, that of the grazing, hoofed herbivores such as horses and cattle.

As these two expansions took advantage of new physical and biologic opportunities, a third trend subdivided ways of life so that, by becoming more specialized within an environment, more species could occupy that environment. Terrestrial mammals have proliferated by adapting to a wide variety of habitats such as forests, deserts, mountains, tundra, and grasslands, as well as by subdividing the available food within a given habitat by becoming herbivores (cattle), carnivores (cats), scavengers (hyenas), omnivores (primates), grain-eaters (rodents), and insectivores (shrews). Further increase of species within any one of these feeding types is accomplished by specializing in food of a particular size or variety. For instance, some herbivores graze on grasses while others browse on leafy vegetation.

Changes in environment may cause major migrations of organisms, which place new demands on both the invaded and invading species. Periods of great crustal activity accompanied by large shifts in the positions of the lands and seas have put great stress on past terrestrial and marine communities. Life has not just been a passive participant in earth history, however. For as life has evolved it has brought about significant changes in the earth's condition. Thus, the appearance and evolution of photosynthesizing plants altered the original atmosphere from one rich in carbon dioxide, methane, and ammonia to one predominantly composed of nitrogen and oxygen. The tremendous storehouse of energy provided by the fossil fuels—oil, gas, and coal—is, of course, also a result of past animal and plant activity.

Man's increasing demands on the earth's environments for providing resources and storing wastes have seriously impaired or even destroyed many animal and plant communities and their habitats. These losses not only may be aesthetic, which is serious enough, but they may even threaten our future survival. For example, the destruction of coastal marshes not only results in the loss of a natural environment, but, because the marshes are sources of nutrients as well as spawning grounds and nurseries for shallow offshore marine life, their destruction diminishes the food resources of the sea at a time when rapidly increasing population requires larger marine harvests.

human evolution

Man's early ancestors, the *australopithecines,* appeared roughly 2 million years ago in Africa. They had evolved from a line of ground-dwelling, vegetarian, apelike creatures. The major distinction between these early proto-humans and their primate predecessors was the shift to hunting small game in open grasslands. Occupation of this ecologic niche was chiefly accomplished by behavioral modifications, the most important of which was using tools for capturing and killing game.

For several hundred thousand years, early man slowly improved his adaptation as a hunter by developing more elaborate cultural behavior, including socialization, prolonged rearing of offspring, verbal communication, and tool-making technology. This cultural evolution was accompanied by changes in brain size and in the structure of the face and hands. This stage of man-the-hunter lasted until the end of the last ice age, about 10,000 to 12,000 years ago (Figure 2-10).

During most of this time man was well integrated with his environment. His population was small, probably less than a few million persons, and stable. Hunting pressure on animal game was not significant, although there is some indication that toward the end of this period, when hunting techniques had greatly improved, humans brought some of the larger mammals to extinction. Some of the human cultures of this time hunted solitary game in the forests or caught fish, but again this caused little damage to the environment.

About 8000 B.C., after the end of the last ice age, a number of human cultures developed the practices of crop cultivation and animal domestication. These were some of the most significant cultural changes in all human history. From these practices came large and reliable sources of food, not only permitting a rapid increase in population, but also providing enough of a surplus that some members of the society could become full-time artisans, soldiers, scholars, and political and religious leaders. The eventual rise of cities and civilization depended on such food surpluses.

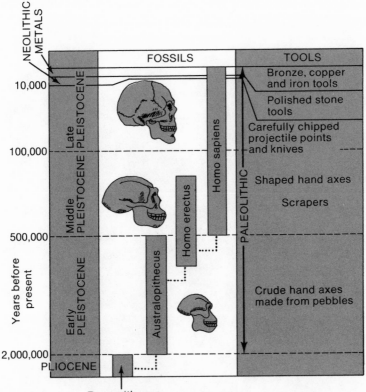

Figure 2-10. The evolutionary stages of man during the Pleistocene and Holocene epochs. Note the changes in skull shape, particularly the flattening of the face and the increase in relative brain cases. Cultural evolution as recorded by tools is also shown. Paleolithic man was a hunter and gatherer; Neolithic man was a cultivator of crops and domesticator of animals. SOURCE: A. McAlester, *The History of Life* (Prentice-Hall, Inc., Englewood Cliffs, N.J., 1968), p. 142.

To cultivate plants and raise livestock, humans felled forests to clear the land, dammed streams and rivers for irrigation, and altered the natural environment in many other ways. Humans were now well on their way to becoming, for the first time in their history, a significant factor in the earth's environment. Just how significant an agent humans have become, and in how astonishingly short a time, is considered next.

These arguments regarding man's dominion over nature miss the point, for several reasons. First, the environmental impact of a single human action, such as planting an acre of corn, commuting to work by car, or throwing the air-conditioner switch, is small in itself, yet the total regional or even global impact of these activities by thousands or millions of persons can be enormous. (Consider the Oklahoma "dust bowl" of the 1930's, the air pollution in the Los Angeles area, or the recurring power shortages in New York City.)

Second, we must evaluate the impact of human activities on the natural environment over an interval of time. Thus, farming or burning fossil fuels can, over a period of years, significantly alter the landscape or change the composition of the atmosphere.

Third, new advances in technology have provided humans with the power to make large, instantaneous changes in the environment, especially through the production of nuclear energy. The ability to concentrate and release tremendous amounts of energy in a relatively small area within just a few seconds has given man's impact on the natural world a whole new dimension, unforeseen just a few decades ago (Table 3-1).

Finally, the fact that humans have the power to alter the natural environment is not necessarily intrinsically "bad." The really crucial issue is *how, when,* and *where* this power is exercised. With the rate of energy consumption in the United States doubling every 10 years, with the world population doubling every 35 years, and with American cities doubling in area every few decades or less, it is clear that the growth in population and technology now has, and will continue to have, a considerable impact on the natural world, both locally and on a global scale.

In this chapter we discuss some examples of human interaction with the land; that is, we compare some of our human activities with natural processes. Like the history of the earth, the history of man reveals an endless sequence of change and modification of the earth's surface. Today the rate of man-made change may be increasing spectacularly in some parts of the world; elsewhere, however, far less obvious changes wrought by man over long periods of time have resulted in permanent, irreversible alterations of the natural scene.

Human activities are diverse, and we choose to examine briefly

3

man's role in changing the land

Throughout history the impact of human activity on the natural environment has been earnestly debated. Some people have viewed man as the pinnacle of Creation, and, consequently, have assumed that we humans have not only the power to rule the natural world, but even a mandate to do so. This attitude implies that human activities in the natural world are truly significant, and our potential ability to modify the earth is great.

Other people have held the opposing view that humans could modify the earth here and there, but the global scale of these changes is quite small, and the powers at our command are puny compared with natural forces. For example, it seems inconceivable that any human change would compare with the natural forces responsible for the Grand Canyon.

TABLE 3-1. ENERGY RELATIVE TO USSR
1961 H-BOMB

Event	Relative energy	Absolute energy (ergs)[a]
Santorin ("Atlantis"?) volcanic eruption and tsunami; prehistoric	1880x	4.5×10^{27}
Tambora, Indonesia volcanic eruption; 1815	583x	1.4×10^{27}
Mt. Mazama-Crater Lake, Oregon, volcanic eruption; prehistoric	283x	6.8×10^{26}
Average hurricane, 24-hour period	158x	3.8×10^{26}
Krakatoa, Indonesia, volcanic eruption; 1883	75x	1.8×10^{26}
Alaska earthquake; 1964[b]	2x	5.0×10^{24}
SOVIET H-BOMB. Novaya Zemlya; 1961	1	2.4×10^{24}
Surtsey, Iceland, volcanic eruption; 1963	5/6x	2.0×10^{24}
San Francisco earthquake; 1906	3/4x	1.8×10^{24}
Arizona meteorite; prehistoric	1/32x	7.6×10^{22}
Average thunderstorm	1/250x	1.0×10^{22}
US A-BOMB, Hiroshima; 1945	1/2900x	8.4×10^{20}

[a]An erg is a unit of energy; 1 ton of TNT releases 4.2×10^{16} ergs.

[b]Energy released during the initial shock was about one-quarter the total energy.

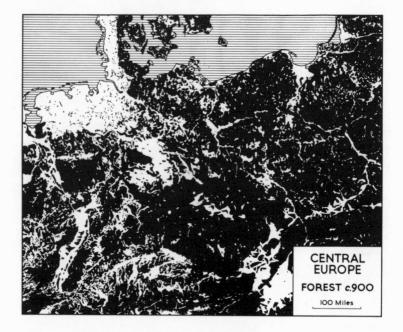

Figure 3-1. Maps of north-central Europe showing changes in vegetation between 900 and 1900 A.D. with a reduction in forested areas from about 80 percent to about 24 percent. SOURCE: W. Thomas *et al., Man's Role in Changing the Face of the Earth* (University of Chicago Press, Chicago, 1956), pp. 202-203.

a few that are most closely related to the natural environment. These include agriculture, mining, engineering and construction, the exploitation of groundwater, and interaction with other living species. Our objective is to show how each of these activities is intricately bound up with natural processes and phenomena, and, that to understand fully their impact on the environment, they must be viewed in their geologic context.

FORESTS, FIELDS, AND FARMS

Human influence on the world's vegetation has been so pervasive that we do not know what the earth's landscapes looked like before man's advent. Ever since the mythical Promethean gift of fire— evidence of which is found in the charcoal hearths of Peking Man

CENTRAL
EUROPE

FOREST c.1900

100 Miles

—some hundreds of thousands of years ago, man has used fire not
only for heat, light, and cooking, but also for removing underbrush
to improve visibility and mobility when hunting, for increasing
grassland for pasturage, and for clearing forests to use the fertile
soil for farming.

deforestation

Hence, from earliest times humans have reduced the area of forests,
replacing them with grasslands and farms. In recent years the pace
of forest destruction has accelerated as the demand for forest products, such as charcoal, lumber, and pulpwood, has increased. The
extent of the destruction is exemplified by the fact that in 900 A.D.
central Europe, north of the Alps, was at least 80 percent forest,
whereas by 1900 A.D. only 24 percent was forest (Figure 3-1). In
northwestern Europe, the destruction of forests created an environment capable of supporting large human populations, necessary for
the flourishing of complex civilization. Here also, intensive agriculture, coupled with heavy animal manuring, has made the cleared
land even more fertile than the original forest soils it replaced.

The history of forest destruction has not been a steady one. When civilization declined or contracted, as in the Roman Empire after the fourth century A.D., forests reclaimed the abandoned fields. But after about 1500 A.D., in central and western Europe, timber shortages became widespread and once again the forests were cut back. As the forested areas shrank, and thus became more valuable, the state or ruling class often made provision for their preservation, even in the face of strong opposition from the peasantry.

However, the area of forest in other parts of the world seems to be increasing. Certainly it has done so in the last one hundred years in the eastern United States. Late in the nineteenth century as much as 80 to 90 percent of the forests in central and southern New England were felled for farms, pastures, or lumber. Today, 70 to 80 percent of Massachusetts, for example, has been returned to forest. The tree species are mostly the same as before, except for the absence of the scattered, huge white pines of the pre-Colonial forests.

effects of deforestation

Given the overall history of deforestation, we might ask what its geologic significance has been. Forest soil and the vegetative litter on it readily absorb rainfall, which either infiltrates to the groundwater reservoir below or is transpired into the atmosphere by living plants. Consequently, except in unusually heavy rains, water flow in the streams that drain forested regions is moderated and evenly distributed throughout the year. Because of the greater circulation of groundwater, the forest tends to help soil development, and the reduction in surface water flow reduces the rate of soil erosion. Thus, forested areas tend to have thick soils, relatively great physiographic stability, and low erosion rates.

In other regions, particularly those with highly seasonal rainfall and periodic, or irregular, drought, the destruction of forests has resulted in the deterioration of the land's ability to support human or other animal life. Such a situation arises when the soil loses nutrients because of its deteriorating capacity to absorb water and because of rapid soil erosion, which leaves behind bare bedrock.

Forest cutting has not always resulted in permanently cleared areas. In tropical forested regions humans practice various forms of shifting cultivation (so-called "slash-and-burn farming"). That is, a small patch of forest is cleared and burned, and the mineral nutrients of the wood ash act as fertilizer. Crops are grown for a few years until the soil fertility is reduced. Then the area is abandoned and grows back into forest while a new clearing is made elsewhere. Such a method of rotating agriculture allows the gradually returning forest to reconcentrate mineral nutrients, thereby regenerating soil fertility.

Historic, botanic, and geographic studies have demonstrated that on every continent vast areas have been cut for agriculture, for pasture, or for timber. Throughout the world much that passes for virgin forest to the untrained eye has, in fact, been cut countless times. In some regions of the world all that remains of the early natural forests are small tracts of wooded groves set aside for religious purposes.

overgrazing

The herding of livestock has also had substantial impact on the world's vegetation because forests were felled to provide additional land for grazing cattle. Certain livestock, notably goats, kept the forest brush from returning. Since the herdsman's interest was in his livestock rather than in the land itself, and since he often measured his wealth in cattle, sheep, or goats, the herds were allowed to increase to the point where they seriously overgrazed the land. If the land became overgrazed, the herdsman would move on to new land, while the overgrazed land suffered severe erosion and deterioration. Such overgrazing probably played an important part in the decline of some of the ancient Middle Eastern civilizations. It certainly was a critical factor in the ruin of much Spanish agricultural land in the late fifteenth and early sixteenth centuries, the effects of which are still evident today.

Not all vegetational changes and their accompanying influences on soil building or soil erosion can be solely attributed to humans. Natural fluctuations in climate can cause significant shifts in vegetation. Since the end of the last glacial age, some 10,000 years ago, there have been major changes in worldwide patterns of vegetation. Some of the world's widespread grasslands are not due to human use of fire to burn forests for making grassland; rather, there is reliable geologic evidence that some types of natural grasslands have been part of the world's landscapes tens of millions of years before man's appearance on earth.

MAN AND OTHER LIVING CREATURES

Not only have humans modified the land for agriculture and pasturage, but they have also markedly altered the animals and plants that live on it. Our expanding human population has required more and more land for raising food, space to live, transportation routes, commerce, mining, and recreation. The consequent landscape alteration has usually resulted in such drastic environmental changes that the natural flora and fauna have been greatly reduced in numbers and in kinds, if not exterminated altogether.

extinction

Man-induced extinction or restriction of other organisms is certainly not a recent phenomenon. There is evidence that throughout our history we have exerted great pressure on many local animal and plant communities. For example, in late Pleistocene time the extinctions of many large, hoofed herbivores (wooly mammoth and mastodon), and the large carnivores that preyed upon them (sabertooth tiger) are thought by some scientists to be the result of excessive hunting by prehistoric man.

Humans have not only exterminated some animals and plants, they have also brought about large increases in the numbers and geographic ranges of others. For instance, the disturbance of natural plant communities such as forests and grasslands by agriculture has resulted in the increase and spread of other species, some desired (the crop itself) and some undesired (various weeds). In a similar fashion, rodents like the common rat have accompanied man's worldwide expansion. Of course, the breeding and raising of livestock, such as chickens, pigs, goats, sheep, and cattle, have greatly increased the numbers and varieties of these species.

Although we are becoming aware of our role in the elimination of some organisms and the proliferation of others, we cannot predict with certainty what the full ecologic consequences might be.

In several cases the extinction of animals or plants is, if nothing else, an aesthetic loss. However difficult such judgments are to evaluate, most people would agree that the loss of wild herds of buffalo, large flocks of passenger pigeons, and great stands of virgin redwoods is hardly offset by the spread of rats, cockroaches, starlings, and ragweed, even though they might disagree about the relative value of the increase of corn, hogs, and cattle. Aesthetics are certainly important, but changes in natural communities ought to be considered from points of view other than, simply, that the extermination of a species is "bad." For, indeed, the history of life indicates that the extinction of species is almost universal. Of all past species, more than 99 percent have become extinct, either by complete extermination or by evolution into new forms. However, present rates of extinction are much faster today than before man's appearance.

preserving diversity

There are sound biological reasons for trying to preserve the abundance and variety of life on earth, even if it may be difficult to demonstrate that any *particular* species must be protected on ecologic grounds alone. After all, much of the understanding of our own species depends on studies of other animals. For example, much of our knowledge of the laws of genetics that apply to all organisms comes from a half century of studying the common fruit fly. Recent behavioral studies of chimpanzees indicate the crucial role of physical affection during infancy in preventing certain kinds of emotional disturbance in later life, an observation that presumably also applies to humans. Another reason for protecting the diversity of life is that many early domesticated plants and, more recently, useful medicinal plants, have been derived from a wide variety of wild species; hence, natural populations of animals and plants may provide a valuable "genetic bank" from which we may have to draw in the future.

Many biologists think that diversity of species is, in itself, ecologically important because a complex ecological system, composed of many interacting species, tends to be more stable and less vulnerable to environmental disturbances. By contrast, simple ecological systems in which just a few species interact with each other tend

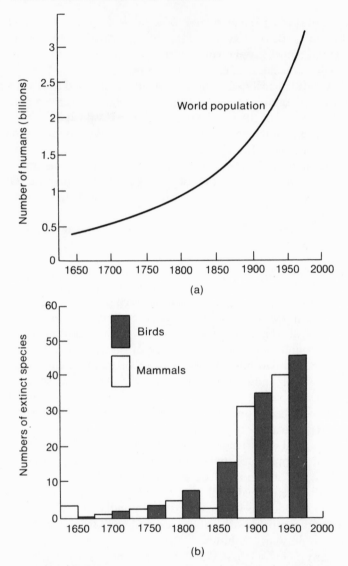

Figure 3-2. Geometric increase in the human population (a) paralleled by increasing numbers of extinctions in birds and mammals (b). Although the close parallelism of these two curves does not in itself prove cause and effect, it suggests that as man's numbers increase, more and more living species become exterminated. SOURCE: V. Ziswiler, *Extinct and Vanishing Species* (Springer-Verlag, New York, 1967).

to be more susceptible to serious disruption by environmental fluctuations. Thus, farms or fields planted with only one or two
are fairly easily invaded by insect pests because many of the
natural predators were eliminated during the initial clearing (
land. For this reason, among others, many European farmers
retained some of the original vegetation along the edges o
cultivated land. These "hedge rows" provide a natural habita
a large variety of animals that help to keep the cultivated port
of the land more pest-free than they would be otherwise.

When we think of the increase in human populations and
intensive use of land, perhaps we should not be surprised that
rise in world population appears to be paralleled by an increase
the number of extinct species (Figure 3-2). If we could extend
graph even farther back in time, when man became first a hun
and later a farmer, the curve might show several periods of rap
extinction separated by plateaus during which extinctions we
relatively few. It is apparent, however, that with the technolo
available to us today we need to have a much more watchful e
over our fellow creatures with whom we share this earth, if we wish
to preserve the biologic and aesthetic values of natural flora and
fauna. For animals and plants, too, are nonrenewable, irretrievable
resources.

MINES AND QUARRIES

The significance of mineral products in the development of civilization is clearly apparent from such expressions as "the Stone Age,"
"the Bronze Age," "the Iron Age," and "the Nuclear Age." We
should be aware that bronze has not superseded stone, nor the
atom iron; on the contrary, all these materials—along with more
than a hundred other mineral products—are being used every day
around the world.

mineral production

Each year new mineral products are being developed and introduced into the world's markets with the result that the demand for
minerals is growing at an increasing rate. In the Stone Age, roughly
10,000 years ago, each human probably used no more than a few
pounds of rocks every year for his stone axes and scrapers. Today,

the annual per capita use in the United States of rock, sand, and gravel is nearly 20,000 pounds (more than 9000 kilograms), and this does not include the various metals and other industrial minerals that require mining of many more tons per person of ore-bearing rock.

Virtually all the mineral products we use are produced from mines or quarries. Since these minerals are nonrenewable resources, the mines and quarries are eventually exhausted, leaving behind large holes in the ground often surrounded by great piles of rock rubble. Consequently, the landscape alteration and habitat modification brought about by mining and quarrying are more devastating and more permanent than what results from lumbering or farming.

mineral consumption and dispersal

The materials that are mined or quarried, although ultimately "used up" or "consumed" by humans, do not really disappear; rather, they are transformed into products that are discarded, dispersed, or changed into other "unusable" forms, and sooner or later find their way back into the natural environment. Consider the element boron, for example. This element of "1000 uses," which has worldwide commercial distribution, is mined primarily in California from borax deposited in old salt lakes. Boron is used in eye-drops and various other medicines, in laundry products, as a gasoline additive, as a preservative in jams and jellies, in oven-proof glassware, in the lenses of astronomical telescopes, in termite-proofing compounds, and in machine tools. But after these "1000 uses," large and small, almost none of the boron is readily recoverable. The medicines enter the water cycle either through the tear ducts or elsewhere; the jams and jellies go through the digestive system; the antitermite compounds are eventually leached from building foundations and also pass into the water cycle. So, ultimately, the boron, like many other mineral products, reaches the sea and becomes dispersed.

Not only the product, but the source itself, is a matter of environmental concern. The open pits where much of the borax is mined require the removal of more than 100 feet (over 30 meters) of rock and soil overburden in order to reach the boron-bearing deposits.

By such mining and mineral-production operations, humans become significant agents of environmental change, both in the earth-moving required for mining and in the dispersal of boron from its concentrated state in nature to its final disposal as a waste product.

impact on landscapes

The environmental impact of mining and quarrying is increasing because of the trend away from underground mining to open-pit mining at the earth's surface. Because of lower operating costs, poorer grades of ores, and easier availability of ore, more than 90 percent of the mineral production in the United States today comes from open-pit operations, as compared to a century ago, when most mining was underground. Although the current area occupied by open-pit mining in the United States is less than 0.5 percent, and elsewhere in the world is even smaller, the local impact on the landscape is considerable. Surface mining operations are unsightly and noisy, and the disturbance of the natural ground cover can greatly increase local erosion. The piles of rock and soil removed as overburden from ore-bearing deposits are easily eroded, so local streams and rivers may be seriously overloaded with sediment. Because local habitats will certainly be modified, animal and plant populations are also likely to be affected. Hence, even though the environmental impact of mining and quarrying is localized within relatively small areas, the increasing demand for minerals will spread the impact of mining and quarrying around the world, thus making it a matter of global as well as local concern.

copper: an example

The world's nations can be divided into three categories based on the present and projected amount of their mineral consumption (Table 3-2). Per capita consumption rates in Latin America, Africa, and Asia are only about one-fiftieth that of North America or Western Europe. Today, two-thirds of the world gets along on only about one-quarter of a pound per person per year. If everyone in the world were to consume copper at a rate equal to that of a U.S. citizen—14 pounds (over 6 kilograms) annually—mining operations would have to expand about 50 times!

TABLE 3-2. INCREASE IN WORLD CONSUMPTION OF SELECTED METALS DURING THE 1960s

Metal and year	Group I (Western World)			Group II (Eastern World and Japan)			Group III (Third World)		
	Population (millions)	Metric tons used (thousands)	Pounds per person	Population (millions)	Metric tons used (thousands)	Pounds per person	Population (millions)	Metric tons used (thousands)	Pounds per person
Copper									
1961	543	3280	13.3	403	925	5.1	2115	267	0.28
1969	646	4140	14.2	500	1770	7.8	2704	359	0.27
Aluminum									
1961	543	3070	12.5	403	1117	6.5	2115	201	0.21
1969	646	6140	21.0	500	2320	10.2	2704	525	0.43
Phosphate rock									
1961	543	23,200	105.0	403	8060	44.0	2115	8130	9.50
1968	634	43,000	151.0	487	20,300	92.0	2623	19,800	16.70

As consumption of a particular metal increases, sources of lower and lower grade ore must be sought. Currently, the average grade of copper produced in the United States is about 0.6 percent, so each ton of ore yields about 12 pounds (roughly 5.5 kilograms) of copper. Already some copper mines are operating with ore one-half that grade; and in another decade the grade may be further reduced to 0.25 percent, even without a large increase in demand, owing to the depletion of higher grade ore deposits. When the time comes —and it may not be far away—that the world must obtain its copper from 0.2 percent ore, then 10 times as much rock will be mined to produce the *same* amount of copper as was produced in 1910 when the ore grade was 2 percent. If we further assume that the 4 billion people in the world in 1980 will use the same amount of copper that people in the western world now use, approximately 13 billion metric tons of ore will have to be produced.

To visualize how large an amount of ore this is, we can consider one of the largest open pit mines in the world, the Bingham copper mine of Utah. In the last half-century or so this mine has produced nearly 1 billion metric tons of ore and has left a hole in the ground 2 miles (3.25 kilometers) long, 1.5 miles (nearly 2.5 kilometers) wide, and almost 0.5 mile (0.75 kilometer) deep (Figure 3-3).

To produce 14 pounds (about 6 kilograms) of copper per person, seven or eight open-pit mines the present size of the Bingham mine would have to be excavated *each year* to provide the required amount of copper ore! Man would then most certainly be a significant "geologic agent," especially when we realize that, at present, the mining and mineral wastes produced each year in the United States amount to 1.5 billion metric tons, more than three times the annual sediment load of the Mississippi River.

The environmental impact of mining and quarrying is subject to some modification and management. To date, however, the side effects of mining and quarrying have often included sinking of the land—sometimes up to several feet—the fouling of hundreds of miles of waterways by highly acidic waters drained from mines, and the transportation and deposition of hundreds of thousands of tons of sediment eroded from open pits, quarries, and piles of waste rock. In forested regions the sediment eroded from strip mines exceeds by 1000 times the quantity of sediment usually transported by undisturbed streams. Thus, although far less extensive than

Figure 3-3. Oblique aerial view of the Bingham Canyon Copper Mine in Bingham, Utah. This is one of the largest man-made excavations on the earth's surface. SOURCE: Courtesy of Kennecot Copper Corporation.

agriculture in area, the environmental impact of mining and quarrying can be truly significant.

CONSTRUCTION

To many, mining and quarrying seem to be destructive activities, for they involve the removal and disintegration of vast quantities of the earth's crust. Almost all our other engineering activities are viewed more positively and are generally referred to as "construction." The building of highways and cities, the installation of power plants, the erection of dams, and the excavation of tunnels and canals are all viewed as constructive. But these activities also have directly observable natural effects, at times on a scale much larger, and with more environmental impact, than mining or quarrying. Lake Mead behind Hoover Dam, for example, occupies an area of 227 square miles (nearly 600 km²) in what was previously desert land. (Lake Mead is small compared with an ancient lake that once covered the region, several million years before the desert was there; in a way, then, an earlier natural environment has been partially restored. This example poses an interesting paradox for environmentalists.)

impact on landscapes

Construction may have unanticipated side effects that, though not immediately observable, may eventually produce environmental consequences that are quite serious. For instance, the Aswan Dam in Egypt may well be already having effects on the Nile Delta in that the river's sand and silt are being deposited behind the dam instead of within the delta; the result is that the delta, and even much of the Palestinian coast, may be severely eroded.

It is difficult, of course, to measure accurately the environmental significance of reshaping the landscape by various construction activities. Yet we are all familiar with the vast expanses of bare rock and loose soil that are exposed during the construction of shopping centers, new houses, and highways. For the United States in the past decade, the land area stripped by urban construction is about 630 square miles (over 1600 km²) per year. Since roughly 4500 metric tons of sediment are produced for each square mile (2.5 km²) of land exposed during construction, these 630 square miles have yielded nearly 3 million metric tons of new sediment each year, or 1.5 times the annual sediment load carried by the Potomac River. Urban expansion along the Atlantic seaboard results in an annual increase of 2 tons of sediment for each new person added to the urban population. For every mile (1.6 kilometers) of two-lane highway constructed, about 35 acres (14 hectares) of land are cleared. In the last 10 years approximately 800,000 miles (1,287,000 kilometers) of highway have been built, thereby exposing to severe erosion more than 43,000 square miles (111,000 km²) of surface area. The sediment eroded and redistributed by all these constructive activities causes, among other things, silting of reservoirs used for water supply and recreation, filling of marshes along the coast, and elimination of spawning grounds for fish and other aquatic animals.

environmental feedback

One natural environment that has been especially modified by human construction is the river flood plain. From the earliest days of civilization, humans have settled on the flood plains of the world's rivers because the soil was rich, deep, and easy to cultivate, because transportation from place to place was greatly simplified,

Figure 3-4. In June 1972, flood waters from Hurricane Agnes inundated the Governor's Mansion in Harrisburg, Pennsylvania. SOURCE: Wide World Photos. (Photos of this flood were unavailable from the Pennsylvania Geological Survey because their library had been flooded.)

and because there was always plenty of fresh water for drinking, irrigation, or industry. The major drawback of living on a river flood plain is the constant threat, and occasional reality, of a major flood (Figure 3-4). Because of the great investment of labor and capital in establishing human settlements along rivers, we have had to put still more energy and money into preventing floods that would destroy what we have built. Consequently, artificial levees have been constructed to confine flood-swollen rivers, and dams have been built upstream to catch water during times of heavy runoff for later release during the year when water might be in short supply. These preventive and protective measures, many of them undertaken years ago, have effects that are only now being fully recognized.

Sediments previously deposited over the river flood plains, and now held back by dams and levees, no longer are bringing nutrients to the farmland adjacent to the rivers. Consequently, artificial fertilizers must be increased to maintain the soil's fertility. At the same time, the dams are holding back sediment that would normally be added to the coastal areas and compensate for the erosion caused by winter storms and longshore currents. For example, in southern California, all the major rivers have been dammed for flood control or to provide reservoirs. Severe erosion along the southern California coast is being temporarily forestalled by the dredging of new small-boat harbors; this dredged sediment supplies the sand and silt formerly brought to the coast by rivers. However, construction of these harbors will not continue indefinitely, and unless drastic measures are taken all the coastal beaches may be lost in as little as 10 years after the dredging stops. The enormous investment of energy and money spent on river modification in flood plain areas therefore may have detrimental effects elsewhere. Before long, we may have to choose between beaches and flood-control and water-storage dams. This situation provides a classic example in which, in one respect, we have achieved phenomenal short-term success as geologic agents without foreseeing the long-term damaging results.

urbanization

Human settlements in other natural environments can have a similar heavy impact on the land. Urbanization in hilly regions, for instance, can greatly modify the natural environment by covering more and more of the terrain with buildings, roads, and other impervious materials. To protect the foundations of these works, various engineering devices ensure that no water enters the ground beneath them. Water falling at higher elevations is carefully diverted to other areas, further downslope. If there is natural, undisturbed land below, the increased runoff may cause a marked increase in erosion or may induce landsliding, depending on the rock and soil conditions. Moreover, the water that normally would have seeped into the rock and soil to the groundwater reservoir is prevented from doing so.

Urbanization has also led to the reclamation of large areas of coastal marshes to provide room for more housing and industry. In the United States alone about 560,000 acres (nearly 227,000 hectares), or 2 percent of our total marshlands, have been filled in the last 20 years. Reduction in marshlands can have a profound impact on the many marine fish and shellfish that depend on them as food sources and spawning grounds. As an example, about 50 percent of the world's commercial fishes spend some part of their lives in coastal marshes and estuaries.

It is also known that many of civilization's past achievements have depended on the reclamation of coastal marshes. The best example is provided by the Dutch, who turned large areas of tidal flats on the North Sea coast into productive agricultural land. In fact, from one-third to one-half of the present area of modern Holland has been reclaimed from the sea. Ancient Rome, too, made use of Etruscan technology in the sixth century B.C. for draining the marshes and building sewers to make the area more suitable for human settlement. Even the filling of the Back Bay marshes of Boston in the nineteenth century played a role in the subsequent development of that city.

GROUNDWATER

Since time immemorial, wells have provided a major source of water in semiarid and arid regions for drinking, irrigation, and, more recently, industry. In its natural untapped state, water from rainfall infiltrating the ground equals the water lost by seepage into rivers and lakes, by evaporation, and by plant transpiration. There is, therefore, a dynamic natural equilibrium between the annual inflow and outflow of groundwater.

salt water intrusion

Along coasts, groundwater has a lower, salt water portion and an upper, fresh water portion. Because of their different densities, the fresh water floats on the salt water. Continuous replenishment, or recharge, of the fresh water provides sufficient volume and pressure to prevent the salt water from rising. Thus balanced, the level of the boundary surface between the fresh water and the underlying salt water tends to remain constant.

When wells are dug to tap this underground fresh water, the dynamic equilibrium between inflow and outflow may be changed, which can result in a significant shift in the fresh water–salt water boundary. If water is drawn from wells in relatively small amounts, the rate of recharge is usually sufficient to maintain the position of the boundary. But if the rate of withdrawal is high, the boundary between the fresh water and salt water will rise closer to the earth's surface and soon the wells will be drawing increasingly saltier water.

Salt water intrusion and the consequent contamination of fresh water are likely to occur in coastal areas with large populations and limited surface water supplies. These problems are already apparent in Long Island, coastal New Jersey, Miami, Houston, Los Angeles, and the Great Valley of California, as well as in Rotterdam, Tel Aviv, Calcutta, Buenos Aires, and elsewhere.

depletion

In interior lands as well as along the coasts, groundwater levels have been considerably altered by our heavy demand for water. When the Great Plains of the United States were first settled people soon discovered that the area was underlain by a vast source of groundwater, the porous Dakota Sandstone. The flowing, fountaining, artesian wells that were developed in the Dakotas and Nebraska, supplying fresh water without pumping, were a boon to further settlement and the establishment of agriculture in an area that was otherwise poor in water. Gradually, however, as more and more of this underground water was withdrawn from the Dakota Sandstone, the water pressure dropped until wells ceased to flow. Today, wells drilled in this area have to go deeper to reach the available water, and expensive pumping is required to draw the water.

The same sequence of events has also occurred in the eastern half of the interior of Australia, which is underlain by a great artesian basin with an enormous reservoir of underground water. Extensive withdrawal of this water by windmill pumps to supply water for cattle and sheep has lowered the pressure so that springs previously found on low mounds rising above the nearly featureless plain have stopped flowing.

subsidence

The water demands of large industries, vast irrigation projects, and great cities in arid regions cannot be met by withdrawing groundwater at the low rates that recharge reservoirs because the amount added to the reservoir is insufficient. In fact, the only way that the cities of Los Angeles and Phoenix, and the great irrigation projects of California and Arizona, were able to be established was by "mining" the groundwater that had been accumulating for hundreds to thousands of years. In these areas groundwater has been pumped out many times faster than it has been replenished by natural recharge. As a result, the water table has dropped many tens of feet, and in some instances, caused the land to subside. In the Santa Clara Valley of California, for example, the ground surface has been lowered as much as 12 feet (3.65 meters) as population and the subsequent water demand have increased (Figure 3-5).

Subsidence following groundwater withdrawal in central California has led to other problems. The Central Valley Project, built in the 1930s, was designed to transport water from the north end of the San Joaquin Valley to irrigate the south end of the valley, about 100 miles (160 kilometers) away. To replace the water that formerly irrigated pastures and fields in the north end of the valley, water from the delta region of the Sacramento River was lifted by pumps and moved southward by gravity in the Delta–Mendota

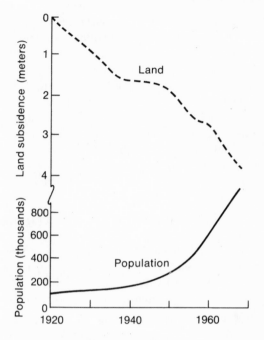

Figure 3-5. Historic trends of population increase and land subsidence in Santa Clara County, California. The growth in population has increased water demand with the result that the area around San Jose has subsided roughly 12 feet (about 4 meters) in the last 50 years. SOURCE: G. Aron and V. Scott, "Dynamic Programming for Conjunctive Water Use," Journal of the Hydrolics Division, Proceedings of the American Society of Civil Engineers, Paper 8145, May 1971, p. 711.

Canal. During the 1940s and 1950s the area crossed by the canal was developed into farmland, irrigated by pumping from underground reservoirs. However, the land subsided along the canal's route as a result of the withdrawal of groundwater; this lowered the canal's gradient and the water formed ponds. Consequently, it is more expensive and more difficult to deliver the water where it's wanted.

Sometimes the rock stratum, or aquifer, that carries underground water is a porous sandstone surrounded by clay-rich layers. When the water is withdrawn from the sandstone, seepage of water from the clays causes them to compact considerably, leading to the subsidence of the overlying ground surface. In Mexico City, for instance, land subsidence has accompanied the withdrawal of water from the extensive aquifer beneath Lake Texcoco, resulting in disturbed building foundations, cracked walls, and ruptured water and sewer mains.

Our extensive use of groundwater has thus made us a major geologic agent. We have, by our heavy withdrawal of groundwater, contributed to subsidence of the land, the lowering of water tables, salt water intrusion into fresh groundwater, and depletion of groundwater at rates faster than it can be naturally replenished.

CONSEQUENCES AND IMPLICATIONS

What can we conclude from this brief summary of man's relation to the land? On what scale do we measure our impact on the earth against that of natural processes? Is there, perhaps, more than just one scale? The following conclusions seem worth considering.

• The surface of the earth, and the animals and plants that dwell on it, have been greatly modified by humans over a period of 15,000 years or less. Certainly since the beginning of civilization, about 6000 years ago, the land's surface has been altered virtually everywhere, and little of what might be called original or untouched nature remains. We are not living upon a pristine earth, but upon an earth already much changed by man.

• Human capacity for modifying the landscape has been growing at a rapid rate. The energy we now have available for all our grand designs and great works vastly exceeds the energy available to primitive man. Thus, our ability to cause change is still greatly increasing.

• Viewed on a geologic scale of time and magnitude, the environmental impact of humans may seem relatively little and the energy at our disposal relatively small compared to the natural processes of erosion, the uplift of mountains, the energy generated in earthquakes, and the volume of material released into the atmosphere by volcanic eruptions.

- Although our modification of the earth is small compared to natural processes, it is not negligible. The impact of many small changes can be cumulative, as in the case of converting forested land to agricultural land. In a similar manner, changes such as the introduction of a new animal or plant to a particular region can trigger far-reaching alteration of the environment. So too, the effects of building cities, mining ore, erecting dams, draining and filling marshes, and withdrawing groundwater have enormous impact at specific local sites. And as such sites are usually closely associated with population centers, they can directly affect the lives and property of millions of people. Obviously, the environmental effects of many human activities are greater on a local scale than when viewed on a global scale.

- Even though we humans are obviously capable of fouling our own nest, we should recognize that natural processes have the same, or even greater, capacity. Thus, while sediment derived from construction can destroy San Francisco Bay or Jamaica Bay, the natural sediment carried by streams and rivers over a long period of time would certainly do the same. Yet we do not have to exaggerate our significance as geologic agents to conclude that our role is sufficiently important that we are capable of degrading and depleting the natural environment by ourselves, often at rates much faster than nature's and with equally lasting effects.

- The geologic record of ancient life provides no evidence that mankind is destined to survive forever on this planet. Indeed, all the evidence is to the contrary, for many more species have become extinct than have survived. Unlike the species that have gone before us, however, we possess the knowledge and capacity to learn to adapt to the finite living space, materials, and energy of the earth well enough to postpone or possibly prevent our own ultimate extinction.

4

land use and misuse

Looking at the natural environment around us, and recognizing that we have already had a tremendous impact on it—sometimes intentionally, often unwittingly—we can focus on a few specific issues where our geologic perspective helps to define the problem, to evaluate its significance, and to suggest possible solutions.

We have chosen four specific topics of current concern: our finite mineral resources, the safe disposal of our ever-increasing wastes, the slow and inexorable erosion of our soils, and the rare but potentially catastrophic geologic hazard. We mine the earth for those minerals so crucial for our civilization, and we bury within it the wastes which civilization produces so abundantly. Wind and water remove, grain by grain, the incredibly thin veneer of soil that covers the earth where we grow our food. And there are other dangers—earthquakes, floods, erupting volcanoes, tsunami, and landslides—of far less frequency which, at one quick stroke, can devastate human life and property. Soil erosion is slowly nibbling us to death; but natural disasters, however sporadic, can devour us in one gulp.

MINERAL DEPOSITS

Ever since primitive man chanced upon a particularly favorable rock and chipped it to form a simple tool, mineral deposits have been used by humans. As soon as that initial tool was discarded and another likely piece of rock was sought to make a second one, primitive man became a prospector. From such humble beginnings has our dependence on mineral deposits grown. Besides providing the natural materials that are the basis of construction, manufacturing, and metallurgical industries, mineral deposits (in the form of fossil fuels, and more recently nuclear fuels) also supply the energy necessary for these industries.

economics of mineral recovery

Virtually all mineral deposits, whether fuels, metals, or industrial minerals, are limited in amount, are nonrenewable on a human time scale, and must be located and mined to be utilized. They have been emplaced by natural processes, usually over a long period of time, and their abundance, location, and grade are not subject to change. Technology, new discoveries, or specific economic and political situations may make "noneconomic" deposits into "economic" ones—or vice versa—but the deposits themselves obviously remain the same.

The relationship between geologic and nongeologic factors in developing a mineral resource is well illustrated by the history of copper mining in Butte, Montana. The initial mining there was from a number of small, high-grade gold mines. Later, an observant geologist noticed that copper minerals were present with the gold. He consolidated the gold mines into a single, large mining operation that also worked the high-grade copper veins. During this stage in Butte's history, any rock containing less than 3 percent copper was considered below ore grade. Eventually, however, with the introduction of modern earth-moving equipment and bulk mining and ore-processing techniques, poorer grade ore could be used profitably. Now, for example, at the Berkeley pit in Butte, metal is being recovered from rock containing as little as 0.2 percent copper, or 4 pounds (2 kilograms) of copper from 1 metric ton of rock, although ore grade is usually closer to 0.6 percent.

Other factors can change the value of a mineral resource even faster than an advance in mining or metallurgical technology. A rise in the price of silver, for example, makes deposits that were previously below ore grade worth mining. Government stockpiling, too, can quickly cause the rapid economic rise or depression of a specific mineral industry. Other governmental actions may also have profound effects—as witness the spectacular development of mineral production in western Australia immediately after the Australian government's repeal of the embargo on the exportation of iron ore. Even though these factors are outside the usual concern of the geologist, they all influence his effectiveness in trying to find adequate mineral resources for society.

growing demand for minerals

Because the technology of our country and that of the rest of the world is ultimately based on minerals, the rates of consumption are high and are steadily increasing. Table 4-1 presents the U.S. production and consumption of some metals and fuels for 1971 with estimates for the year 2000. In those instances in which the consumption is higher than production, the difference is compensated by foreign imports. Except for a few metals, the U.S. must import a substantial portion of its raw materials or finished products. Among the fossil fuels, we have only coal and oil shale in sufficient amount to meet our probable future demands. Despite our dependency on imports of many minerals, the U.S. is the most nearly self-sufficient nation; most other countries are equally or even more dependent on foreign sources of supply. These facts emphasize the importance of effective governmental policy and foreign relations in assuring a continuing mineral supply for all nations, as well as the need for developing greater self-sufficiency whenever possible for each individual nation.

The large demand for metals is paralleled by the demand for

TABLE 4-1. TOTAL ANNUAL U.S. MINERAL SUPPLIES AND USES

	Domestic primary production	Old scrap[a]	Total amount used[b]	Projected primary demand for 2000 A.D.
Aluminum	450,000	160,000	4,947,000	23,800,000
Copper	1,380,000	422,000	2,122,000	4,860,000
Iron	49,000,000	35,400,000	110,200,000	138,000,000
Lead	517,000	450,000	1,207,000	1,390,000
Mercury	597	378	1995	2730
Bituminous coal & lignite	504,000,000	0	504,050,000	900,000,000
Natural gas (dry)	446,000,000	0	465,080,000	1,030,000,000
Petroleum (including natural gas liquids)	508,190,000	0	668,190,000	1,490,000,000
Uranium	9515	0	9515	55,800

[a]Preliminary data for 1971, given in metric tons. SOURCE: First Annual Report of the Secretary of the Interior under Mining and Minerals Policy Act of 1970 (P. L. 91-631); March, 1972.

[b]Including government stockpiling, industry stocks, and exports. The difference between domestic supply and demand is met by foreign imports.

fuels and nonmetallic minerals. In fact, the value of nonmetallic minerals produced in the United States is more than twice that of metals, while the value of fuels produced is about six times as great. The use of cement, sand, clay, sulfur, phosphate, potash, and mineral pigments and fillers is growing, and so far, with these and most other nonmetallics, their supply is met largely from domestic sources.

Given an expanding population and growing rates of use and consumption, within both the developed and developing nations, the demand for minerals will greatly enlarge. To meet this demand we must find and exploit additional mineral deposits, but since these have finite limits, major advances must be made in recovering used metals and curtailing, as much as possible, the use of irrecoverable ones. Recycling of metals, in particular, is an imminent and inevitable next stage in man's long history of metal technology.

rarity of mineral deposits

Individual chemical elements occur in the earth's crust in a wide range of abundance. Some, such as oxygen, silicon, aluminum, and iron, are extremely common, composing about 46, 28, 8, and 6 percent, respectively, of the crust. Others are much rarer and are present only in trace amounts. If we compare the average abundance of some common metals in the earth's crust with their average concentration in ore, we can calculate the enrichment required to make ordinary rock into ore (Table 4-2).

Aluminum and iron, for example, are the most common metals in the earth's crust and have to be enriched by only a factor of several times to reach ore grade. But other metals, like silver or lead, which usually occur only in small amounts, must be enriched some thousand times in order to reach ore grade. This enrichment or concentration of particular elements within the crust is caused by a variety of geologic processes, including special circumstances of weathering and sedimentation at the earth's surface, or precipitation from hot solutions below the surface. These enrichment processes are uncommon events; hence, such naturally enriched rocks are quite limited in supply. Even those mineral deposits that are considered abundant are, in fact, relatively rare in the earth's crust. Coal, the most abundant mineral fuel, is fairly limited in its

TABLE 4-2. ENRICHMENT FACTOR FOR SOME COMMON METALS

Metal	Percent in crust	Percent in ore	Enrichment factor[a]
Mercury	0.000008	0.2	25,000
Gold	0.0000002	0.0008	4000
Lead	0.0013	5.0	3840
Silver	0.00007	0.01	1450
Nickel	0.008	1.0	125
Copper	0.006	0.6	100
Iron	5.2	30.0	6
Aluminum	8.2	38.0	4

[a]The enrichment factor indicates how many times above its average concentration a metal must be in order to be mined.

distribution. Many nations, for example, completely lack this important resource. Not only is the process of coal formation somewhat unusual in itself, but some coal deposits either have already been eroded or are still buried within the earth's crust beyond our reach. So, not only is the process of mineral enrichment relatively rare, but this rarity is compounded by subsequent loss through erosion or by inaccessibility to human exploitation.

It is difficult to give a precise measure of the rarity of mineral deposits, but the idea may be conveyed indirectly. For example, in the United States during 1966, only 186 mines accounted for over 90 percent of the nation's production of asbestos, bauxite, borax, copper, gold, iron, lead, molybdenum, nickel, phosphate, potash, silver, titanium, tungsten, uranium, and zinc. Among these 186 mines are 3 gold mines, 33 copper mines, 37 lead and zinc mines, 4 molybdenum mines, and 45 iron mines. The number of mines is small, not because additional sources were not sought and developed, but because the total number of deposits is limited and the deposits still undiscovered are increasingly difficult to find.

United States oil field exploration statistics illustrate the increasing difficulty of finding mineral deposits. In 1946, 31 exploratory wells were required to find one that would have a reservoir of at least 1 million barrels of oil; by 1964, 59 exploratory wells were necessary to find a similar reservoir.

This rarity of mineral deposits can be expressed in still another way. For many years the world's principal source of elemental sulfur was from the sulfur deposits associated with subsurface salt domes in the Gulf Coast region of the United States. In 1960, 277 salt domes were known, and of these only 24 had associated sulfur deposits of sufficient size for sulfur recovery. Salt dome deposits are themselves rare, and only 1 in 10 of these rarities had minable sulfur. In 1967, sulfur production was started from surface strata of gypsum and salt in west Texas. These strata cover approximately 90,000 square miles (over 230,000 km^2), but minable sulfur is known to occur only within 2 square miles (5 km^2).

the search for minerals

Because mineral deposits are rare, slow to form, and finite, new ones must be found to replace those being consumed. The rich mineral deposits at the earth's surface have been largely discovered; therefore, we have to seek those which are more deeply hidden within the earth or otherwise obscure. The search for mineral deposits that are not readily apparent has been going on for years, and many subsurface ore bodies have been found and developed. Many more, presumably, remain to be discovered by using the knowledge and techniques of geology and geophysics. At the same time, mining engineers are improving recovery and processing methods to permit the development of already known but lower-grade deposits.

Through technological advances, new ore deposits have been located in areas that were previously combed by countless prospecting geologists. For example, the recent discovery of deeply buried iron ore in southeastern Missouri occurred after an airborne magnetometer survey of the region; similar techniques led to the discovery of iron ore at Sturgeon Lake, Canada. Careful geologic study resulted in finding the Kalamazoo copper ores that lay 0.5 mile (0.8 kilometer) below barren rock in Arizona as well as the new zinc deposits in central Tennessee that were discovered under 1500 feet (457 meters) of unmineralized rock.

Additional mineral deposits will undoubtedly be found with the help of improved exploratory techniques, although no new major technological breakthroughs are anticipated. Geophysical instruments for probing deeper into the earth's crust are needed now, as are devices that can differentiate between various sorts of electrical conductors, that is, that can distinguish ore minerals from other types of minerals. A better understanding of the subtle geochemical differences indicative of mineralization will also greatly help in locating subsurface ore bodies.

Wherever the search for mineral deposits leads us, the ultimate proof of our efforts will be provided by drilling and sampling, which is the most costly part of mineral exploration. Here we can apply new research to interpret drilling results and thus convert "near misses" into important mineral discoveries.

Discoveries resulting from new knowledge and new techniques should not mislead us into thinking that more elaborate technology and more geologic study will always provide us with whatever minerals we might need in the future. We are faced with the hard reality that mineral deposits are finite. Sooner or later we will have to extend the "life" of processed minerals, especially metals, by widespread, large-scale recycling of used materials.

WASTES AND POLLUTION

Perhaps the one environmental concern that is most notorious today is pollution. Despite all the words we hear about pollution, it is rarely defined. Often pollution seems to be equated with wastes of all sorts. Yet that implied definition must be inaccurate because we don't consider the millions of pounds of waste matter annually produced by sea lions and seals along the California coast as "pollution," nor, when romanticizing the rural past, do we view the farmers of the last century as polluting their local streams and rivers.

impact on natural systems

The crucial distinction is that pollution represents an imbalance between waste materials put into a natural system and the capacity of that system to absorb, transport, degrade, dilute, or disperse those materials, with the result that the physical, chemical, or biological characteristics and functions of the system are significantly impaired. If the amount of waste is small relative to the natural reservoir into which it is placed, or if the rate of removal or dilution is equal to the rate of introduction, then we do not normally consider those materials as pollutants.

The wastes introduced into the natural environment by a marble quarry in Vermont, by the burning of raked leaves in a Midwest suburb, by the spilling of gas from one outboard on a Wyoming lake, or by the exhaust of a car climbing the Sierra slopes, are sufficiently small that the natural systems can absorb them. So it is not the wastes themselves that are usually the problem, but the great volume and rate of introduction that has accompanied the rapid increases in population and technology.

In many instances, pollution may be defined as "a resource out of place." Rather than viewing abandoned automobiles, discarded beer cans, or junked appliances as pollutants, we might consider them as a valuable supply of metals that can be recycled. Similarly, treated sewage could be a valuable source of fertilizer if returned to the land, rather than a pollutant when channeled to fresh water and the sea. Although the issue is far from simple, certainly a great deal of the difficulty of solid- and liquid-waste disposal would be reduced if it were seen instead as raw material for recovery and utilization.

natural pollutants

Even without human activity the environment experiences changes caused by the introduction of materials from outside individual natural systems or cycles. For instance, rain and snow carry to the earth millions of tons of salt that has been transported from the oceans' surface into the atmosphere over the lands. Volcanic eruptions have put more dust and gas into the air than have all human activity. Many springs bring enormous quantities of salts and acids into the surface waters. Rivers are the natural transport systems for sediment and chemicals, and the sea is the sump for virtually all the geologic transportation processes occurring on land. The difference between natural sources of wastes and man-made sources is that while we have to live with the former we can do something about the latter.

varieties of pollutants

High population densities or certain kinds of industrial and agricultural activities may cause waste materials to overburden natural processes or systems. Surface waters can be polluted in many different ways. These include domestic sewage and other oxygen-demanding materials that may reduce the oxygen content of the receiving waters to the degree that fish and other aquatic life are killed; infectious agents that cause diseases such as typhoid, intestinal disorders, and various viral ailments; nutrients, especially phosphates and nitrates, which cause excessive algal blooms that, in turn, consume oxygen when they decompose after death; organic chemicals such as pesticides, herbicides, and detergents, which are toxic to many forms of aquatic organisms; petrochemicals, salts, acids, and sludges, which can greatly change the water chemistry; sediment from natural as well as man-induced erosion; radioactive substances whose radiation may cause genetic or tissue damage to aquatic life; and heat, which may alter chemical processes in water and physiological activities in organisms, resulting in a deterioration of the environment and death of animals.

Industrial and domestic. The principal sources of man-made liquid wastes are both industrial and domestic, with factories, mills, and refineries producing more than half of the total volume of waste water, biochemical oxygen demand, and settleable and suspended solids. Household waste water, whether it goes into sewers, septic tanks, or directly onto the surface and into the groundwater, accounts for less than half of the total.

Agricultural. Wastes from livestock feedlots and mineral fertilizers washed from soil are the main sources of agricultural water pollution. The wastes from livestock in the United States are estimated to be equivalent to the amount produced by 2 billion people, although most of this waste is returned to the land and so only a part of it actually affects water resources. Mineral fertilizers, particularly those containing nitrogen and phosphorus, pollute natural waters because they greatly increase the production of organic matter, especially algae, which decompose and seriously deplete the oxygen content of the receiving waters. This situation greatly accelerates the natural aging process of lakes and estuaries (called "eutrophication") which results in a stagnant and "dead" water body. Of course, nutrients from sewage also greatly contribute to eutrophication problems.

Sediment resulting from erosion represents the single largest source of solids entering surface waters. Farming and logging increase erosion rates many times over what they are for land with natural cover, while construction may increase erosion rates 1000 times.

Oil and gas.   Accidental spills or intentional discharges of oil from ships, drilling platforms, pipelines, or storage facilities also cause water pollution. Although accidental spills attract the most publicity, they account for less than 10 percent of the 2.1 million metric tons of oil that humans release directly into the world's waters each year. More than 90 percent comes from the normal, everyday handling of oil at oil wells, in tankers and refineries, in gas stations and garages, and in the burning of fuel oil and gasoline where hydrocarbons are emitted into the atmosphere only to be later carried by precipitation into surface waters. About 0.1 percent of the annual crude oil production eventually ends up in the ocean. This means that in 1980, when the world crude oil production reaches roughly 4 billion metric tons per year, approximately 4 million metric tons of it will end up in the sea—double the current amount.

Atmospheric.   The atmosphere, too, is polluted in many urban areas by the large volume of gases released by burning fossil fuels. In the United States, transportation—particularly automotive—is the greatest source of air pollutants, accounting for more than 60 percent by weight of all air pollutants. The burning of fossil fuels, incineration of solid wastes, manufacturing processes, and other kinds of open burning are responsible for the balance of air polluting emissions, which, in order of decreasing abundance, are carbon monoxide, sulfur oxides, hydrocarbons, nitrogen oxides, and fine particles.

solid wastes

We are generating solid wastes at a very rapid rate as tons and tons of consumer goods—many of them packaged in convenient but almost indestructible containers—flood the marketplace, as buildings are demolished, as industries diversify their products, as minerals are mined and processed, and as crops and livestock are raised.

Waste accumulation. In the United States the domestic solid wastes from cities, ranging from milk cartons to refrigerators, amount to 200 million metric tons per year. This figure will grow to more than 300 million metric tons by 1980. (These data are based on estimates of collected solid wastes; the total figure actually may be as much as twice as large.) Nine million cars are junked each year, and industrial solid wastes amount to over 90 million metric tons annually. The waste from mining, milling, and processing of minerals comes to more than 1500 million metric tons per year. Almost 2 billion metric tons of agricultural wastes are produced annually. These include animal and slaughterhouse wastes, and residues from crop and timber harvesting, vineyard and orchard pruning, and greenhouses.

Waste disposal. Most solid wastes are returned to the land simply by being either piled on its surface or buried at a shallow depth. This method of disposing of solid waste does not disperse pollution as widely as a sewer outfall or factory chimney. The reason for this is that the pollutants from solid wastes must be transported by groundwater, which moves very slowly compared to surface water or air. However, the danger of polluting ground and surface waters remains.

The "resources out of place" definition of pollution is especially appropriate for solid wastes; for to use metals only one time after they have been laboriously located, mined, and processed seems extravagant, especially when we consider how quickly our mineral resources are dwindling. Paper, wood, and glass, too, could all be put to good re-use. Obviously, the recycling of much of our solid wastes ought to be a primary goal of municipal and industrial solid-waste management.

Choosing waste disposal sites. For the immediate future, until large-scale methods of collection and recycling are operating nation-wide, most of our solid wastes must continue to be returned to the land. Here, geologic knowledge has special relevance in

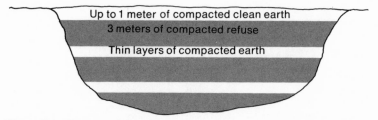

Up to 1 meter of compacted clean earth

3 meters of compacted refuse

Thin layers of compacted earth

Figure 4-1. Cross section of a sanitary landfill where compacted waste is covered each day with several feet of compacted earth. A landfill such as this eliminates the need for burning as well as any problems of odors, flies, or rats. SOURCE: American Chemical Society, *Cleaning Our Environment: The Chemical Basis for Action* (ACS, Washington, D.C., 1969), p. 169.

terms of the kinds of earth materials present at the disposal site, the earth processes operating there, and the length of time that the wastes might constitute a hazard while in the earth. The land and its groundwater vary in their natural capacity to retain, assimilate, or neutralize waste by-products. Therefore, in choosing and operating individual solid-waste disposal sites, careful attention must be paid to existing geologic conditions. Our performance to date has been poor: The disposal sites for 77 percent of all collected solid waste from municipalities in the United States are the 14,000 open dumps scattered all around the country. Only 13 percent of collected waste is deposited in properly operated sanitary landfills where wastes are covered each day with earth (Figure 4-1).

Because we must live close to our solid-waste disposal sites—not only because of the expense of transporting them but also because of the difficulty of putting our garbage near other people—they must be selected to take advantage of the natural protection that the earth can provide. All too often, disposal operations are located in handy, abandoned gravel pits or rock quarries without serious consideration of the likelihood of subsequent pollution.

Climatic factors. Natural controls on the formation and movement of solid-waste by-products are related to climate, earth materials, and the pattern of underground water transport (Figure 4-2). In arid climates, there is not enough rainfall to infiltrate and saturate solid refuse nor to transport the waste by-products through the ground [Figure 4-2(a)]. In humid climates, there is sufficient rain-

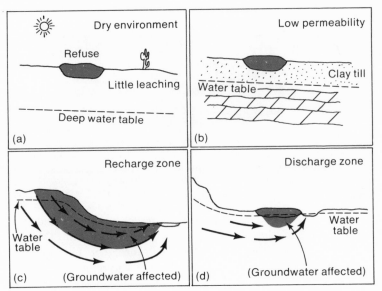

Figure 4-2. Geologic and hydrologic conditions affecting pollution of groundwater from solid waste buried near the land surface. In (a) and (b), the groundwater is protected; whereas in (c) and (d) the groundwater will be polluted by the leachate from the landfill. SOURCE: R. E. Bergstrom, *Disposal of Wastes: Scientific and Administrative Considerations* (Illinois State Geological Survey, Environmental Notes, No. 20, Urbana, Ill., 1968).

fall to saturate the refuse and produce a highly mineralized water called "leachate." In general, the amount of water passing through the refuse is the main control in leachate production.

Groundwater contamination. Leachate, which contains dissolved solids from solid waste, eventually moves into the groundwater. Fine-grained materials, such as clay or silt, transmit groundwater very slowly, usually less than a few feet per year. These materials remove microorganisms from the leachate, often within several feet of the landfill; they also tend to decrease the dissolved chemical content of the leachate [Figure 4-2(b)]. Thus, burying refuse in fine-grained soils or rocks is an effective safeguard against the migration of pollutants, such as pathogenic microorganisms, heavy trace metals, and salts, into the groundwater reservoir. A study of leachate movement from an Illinois landfill showed that the leachate was reduced as much in concentration by passing through 4–5 feet (1–2 meters) of silty clay as by filtering through 600 feet (180 meters) of sand. However, if the underlying soil or rock is too impermeable, the landfill will not drain and the leachate may seep out along the sides of the refuse.

Groundwater movement influences the spread of pollutants from landfills because if refuse is put in a site where water can enter the groundwater below, then the dissolved solids and microorganisms may be carried into the groundwater reservoir [Figure 4-2(c)]. However, if the flow path of the groundwater is long from the point where the leachate enters to the point where wells tap the groundwater, then the leachate contaminants may be removed or reduced to harmless levels. If the disposal site is in an area where groundwater is discharged to the surface, there is less probability of the leachate's entering the groundwater reservoir, but it may enter a nearby body of surface water [Figure 4-2(d)]. These various examples demonstrate the need for us to understand the geology and hydrology of an area before we bury solid wastes in the ground.

Land reclamation. One method of solid-waste disposal currently being considered is to put refuse in abandoned coal strip-mines, although the usual reaction of local inhabitants is that they do not want other people's garbage nearby. Yet the use of solid wastes for reclamation of mined lands (particularly those coal strip-mines where there is not much groundwater flow through the surrounding rocks) is quite feasible and geologically sound in some areas of the country. Until recycling of solid wastes becomes more widespread, we will need more and more land for disposal by burial. Obviously, it is better to *reclaim* land with properly located landfills than to spoil land more suitable for other purposes.

Local geologic and hydrologic conditions are not the only considerations for choosing a site for solid-waste disposal. Economic factors may require that a site be used where conditions are not optimal. In such a case, however, we can install clay liners before disposing of the wastes to reduce infiltration of the leachate into the groundwater reservoir. We can also modify flow systems with drains or pumping to control or redirect leachate movement. And, of course, a waste disposal site ought to be monitored to detect any harmful effects that might develop. All these procedures require an understanding of local geology and hydrology.

liquid wastes

Another method of waste disposal that warrants discussion is the injection, deep into subsurface formations, of liquid wastes from oil field operations and industrial processing (Figure 4-3). In oil fields, many thousands of wells are used for the disposal of brines brought up in oil drilling. Industry uses another 200 wells for the disposal of liquid acid and alkali wastes, pulping liquors, and radioactive uranium mill wastes. These liquids are injected into deep, usually permeable, formations initially filled with groundwater. Rates of injection into these deep formations commonly range from 10 to 300 gallons (about 40 to over 1000 liters) per minute.

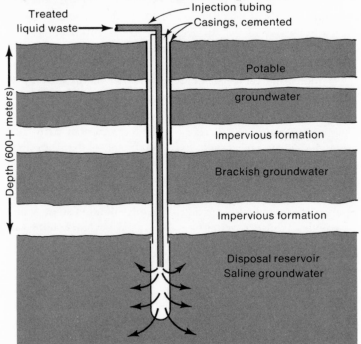

Figure 4-3. Cross section showing a well-injection system for the disposal of liquid wastes in deep, saline, groundwater reservoir. The upward movement of the wastes is prevented by the overlying impervious formations such as shale. The well itself is specially constructed to resist the corrosive action of the waste liquid.

Disposal wells.   As might be expected, certain special geologic and hydrologic conditions are necessary for such disposal wells. The formations into which the wastes are placed must have the kinds of openings that will permit them to transmit the injected liquids, and must be thick and large enough to store them. Sandstones and fractured limestones are the most commonly used rock formations for such disposal well reservoirs. Many sandstones have 10 to 20 percent open pore space, usually filled with water which can be displaced by injected waste fluids. Such reservoir formations should also be overlain and confined by relatively impermeable rocks, such as shale, salt, or gypsum, that will limit the possible upward movement of the wastes. Rock formations filled naturally with saline water are also good barriers because they can accommodate any upward migration of waste fluids, if the formations are thick and porous enough. Usually the potable water within the upper few hundred feet of land surface is separated from the disposal reservoir below it by hundreds to a few thousand feet of intervening rock.

Some problems.   Disposal wells have come to public attention in the recent years as a result of incidents in Colorado and Pennsylvania. In 1967, the use of a 12,000-foot (3600-meter) deep industrial disposal well at the Rocky Mountain Arsenal, near Denver, was halted because the injection of wastes was believed to have triggered a series of earthquakes nearby. In 1968, a disposal well on the shore of Lake Erie in Pennsylvania "blew out," releasing several million gallons of harmful chemicals from a paper plant into the lake. More recently, injection of fluids into the Inglewood oil field in California for secondary recovery of oil is claimed to have activated local faults, resulting in the collapse of the Baldwin Hills water storage reservoir. Partly because of these incidents, and some other failures of brine disposal wells in oil fields, the feasibility of liquid-waste injection into deep formations has been seriously questioned by some geologists and other environmental scientists. At present, however, most industrial and oil field brine disposal wells are operating as designed and without environmental side effects.

Choosing a reservoir.   Disposal wells may be a feasible way of eliminating limited volumes of some kinds of liquid wastes in some areas, but the safety of the technique is proportional to our under-standing of the geologic conditions at the proposed site, the ade-quacy of the engineering, and sufficient monitoring of the injection system to evaluate possible future effects. The injection of liquid wastes into subsurface formations should not be viewed as a quick and easy solution to industrial waste problems. The reservoir space in these formations is limited, inasmuch as the formations are already filled with natural fluids, usually either brine or brackish water. Therefore, space has to be made for the injected wastes by displacement of the naturally occurring fluids, by their compres-sion (which, however slight, in a large volume formation can pro-vide enough additional space to accommodate the waste fluid), and by a slight expansion of the reservoir formation. Space limitations and possible excess pressures are the chief restrictions governing the rate of fluid injection and the volume of fluid that can be placed in a reservoir. Pressure, volume, and movement of the fluids need to be monitored, and the resulting data interpreted in terms of the surrounding geologic conditions.

There is, therefore, a broad range of natural conditions that must be thoroughly considered in determining whether the site of a proposed injection-well system is liable to create hazards to the public or to the successful operation of the system itself. Disposal wells can pose a serious danger in regions where the rocks are fractured or faulted, in areas that are prone to earthquakes, or in places that have been heavily drilled for oil and gas, making it possible for waste fluids to migrate upward through abandoned drill holes. Under favorable geologic and hydrologic conditions, however, and with rigorous, conservative engineering and adminis-trative controls, disposal wells provide an alternative in dealing with some industrial liquid-waste problems by taking advantage of the large reservoir capacity of deeply confined rock formations and the exceedingly slow rate of groundwater movement through the earth.

radioactive wastes

Our expanding industrial and domestic energy demands require increasing reliance on nuclear fuels because the supply of fossil fuels is definitely limited. We may expect that, in the future, more energy will be required for the mining and processing of lower grade mineral deposits and for the large-scale recycling of liquid and solid wastes. However, the radioactive wastes from nuclear power generation constitute a special and a rapidly growing environmental problem. Hence, in our efforts to solve the environmental problems of dwindling high-grade mineral deposits and fossil fuels, we may very well create a new set of environmental problems.

High exposures to radiation are known to be harmful to humans and other organisms, but it is difficult to predict precisely the biological effects of low-level radiation. We are already exposed to low-level radiation from solar cosmic rays that enter the earth's atmosphere and from naturally occurring radioactive substances in the earth's crust. We are also exposed to man-made radiation from medical x rays and radioisotopes as well as from some electronic instruments. We must be careful that radiation from man-made sources does not rise to an unsafe level as the nuclear power industry expands.

Sources.   Radioactive wastes produced by nuclear power generation consist of solids, liquids, and gases that range widely in radiation levels. Radiation is emitted as radioisotopes in the wastes undergo natural decay, so the amount of the radiating material and the level of radiation eventually decrease. Although we may reduce the intensity of radiation by dispersing the radioactive material within a larger volume of nonradioactive material, the process of natural decay is the only way in which radioactivity can be ultimately dissipated. Therefore, the storage of radioactive wastes is only an intermediate step leading to final "disposal" through natural decay.

The largest source of radioactive wastes is nuclear reactors. The heat generated by a nuclear reactor is produced by spontaneous breakdown, or splitting, of the uranium 235 nucleus, so-called "nuclear fission." Some of the breakdown, or fission, products are themselves radioactive. The fuel elements of a reactor accumulate fission products and are chemically processed periodically to recover unused fuel. This operation yields large volumes of liquids containing the fission products and other materials that emit extremely high levels of radiation as well as considerable heat.

Duration.   The storage of radioactive wastes, like the disposal of other wastes, requires rather complete understanding of the earth materials in which the wastes will be stored, the nature and rates of the geologic processes affecting those materials, and the time scale over which those processes are acting. Of particular concern in the storage of radioactive wastes are those radioactive substances having "half-lives" measured in years. A half-life may be defined as the time required for a radioactive substance to decay to one-half its original activity. Thus, a radioactive isotope with a half-life of 10 years will have only half the initial amount of radioactivity it started with after 10 years, one-quarter after 20 years, one-eighth after 30 years, and so on. Short-lived radioactive materials—those with half-lives measured in seconds, minutes, or days—decay fast enough that their existence is fleeting when compared to the time it takes buried containers of radioactive wastes to corrode in the earth, for subsurface water to dissolve the materials containing radioactive isotopes, for moving groundwater to transport radioisotopes to a discharge point at the earth's surface, or for a buried container of radioactive waste to be uncovered by erosion.

Management: dilute and disperse.   Radioactive wastes are managed in three ways: dilute and disperse, delay and decay, concentrate and contain. The first method, dilute and disperse, has been used for the disposal of low-level liquid and gas wastes. At safe levels these wastes are discharged into streams, lakes, or the ocean; with gases, they are released into the atmosphere. The large volumes of water used to cool nuclear reactors, which also contain traces of radioactive substances, are released into large bodies of surface water.

Clays in soils and in stream and lake sediments tend to adsorb and hold radioactive substances being transported in solution, which reduces the mobility of the radioactive materials. This adsorption is an important means of removing radioactive isotopes from low-level waste waters and prevents their spread throughout the natural environment. There may be some danger, however, that concentrations of these adsorbed radioactive isotopes, once extracted, may be released at a later time into the environment by storms, floods, or changes in water chemistry.

Management: delay and decay: The second management method, delay and decay, is used for wastes that contain substantial amounts of short-lived radioisotopes. Low-level solid wastes can be buried at sites where the radioactive isotopes will decay to relatively harmless levels of radioactivity. The sites must be chosen, of course, in such a way that there is virtually no possibility of the radioactive materials' being released before they have decayed sufficiently. Hot wastes produced by the processing of used fuel elements from reactors contain both short- and long-lived radioisotopes and are put in steel and concrete tanks for months to years until their temperature cools and their level of radioactivity diminishes, allowing further handling.

Management: concentrate and contain. The third management method, concentrate and contain, is necessary for high-level radioactive wastes from fuel processing. Millions of gallons of these liquids are produced each year, a small volume compared with the more ordinary municipal and industrial wastes, but nevertheless requiring extensive treatment and storage facilities. The long-lived radioisotopes in these high-level wastes require that they be safely contained for *thousands* of years.

Problems of safety. The possibility of permanent and safe containment of these high-level wastes must become one of our principal environmental concerns. A site of long-term stability for high-level wastes, proposed by the Atomic Energy Commission, is the bedded salt formations, about 1000 feet (over 300 meters) deep, in Kansas. Salt formations are well suited to the storage of such wastes because they are dry and impervious to water, behave plastically under pressure and thus close fractures that might develop, have enough strength to support shafts and rooms during mining, and are good heat insulators. In a carefully selected salt repository wastes would be safe from contaminating the groundwater, would be well below the level of erosion for the required half-million years, would not be likely to be disturbed by any earthquakes, and would have their heat safely contained (Figure 4-4).

Other possibilities for safe long-term storage are injecting liquid

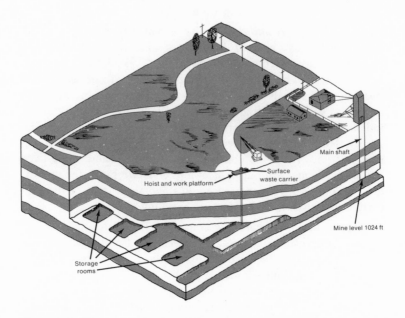

Figure 4-4. Diagrammatic view of the Carey Salt Company mine in Lyons, Kansas, where radioactive waste disposal experiments have been conducted by the Oak Ridge National Laboratory. It is in such a facility as this that high-level radioactive wastes can be stored for extremely long periods of time. SOURCE: C. H. Fox, *Radioactive Wastes* (U.S. Atomic Energy Commission, Division of Technical Information, "Understanding the Atom Series," 1969), Figure 16.

wastes into deep wells; placing liquid wastes in a medium of cement and injecting them into deep shale formations by using high fluid pressures to fracture the otherwise impermeable shale; and storing wastes in man-made caverns deep in rocks other than salts.

These various techniques of radioactive waste storage are appropriate to wastes with different characteristics. Each method, however, should ensure with great certainty that the waste will not find its way into water supplies, or into oil, gas, or other materials that might enter the biosphere within a thousand years or so. This kind of certainty requires detailed knowledge of local geology and hydrology, which normally cannot be obtained without extensive study and testing. Consequently, the choice of sites for nuclear waste storage depends, first and foremost, upon comprehensive geologic information.

SOILS

Soils are obviously important in human affairs because we use them for growing most of our food, all of our wood, and many of our natural fibers. Soils also support the foundations of our highways and other structures as well as provide us with a source of building materials and of mineral deposits. Soils can be viewed from a geologic perspective as products of natural processes working on earth materials over long periods of time, particularly with respect to their initial formation and subsequent management.

soil formation

Soils develop by a complex interaction of the weathering of rock and loose sediments, vegetation, and microorganisms. Climate, topography, and groundwater circulation play major roles, too, as does the length of time available for soil-building processes. Some soils represent unique combinations of all these factors; therefore, they cannot be easily restored for our benefit once they have been destroyed. Other soils are the result of geologic conditions and processes no longer occurring. For example, the fertile soils in the midwestern United States overlie vast quantities of ground-up rock spread by glaciers during the last ice ages, thus forming a mantle of sediment of varying thickness over the underlying bedrock. This mantle consists of unsorted rock debris deposited by glacial ice, beds of sand and gravel laid down by glacial meltwater, and widespread layers of silt blown by winds from river valleys onto the uplands.

Soil types.   These materials, being loose and unconsolidated, were much more susceptible to soil-forming processes following glaciation than was the harder and denser bedrock. Some soils that developed in Michigan and Indiana on limestones laid bare by glacial erosion, about 15,000 years ago, are only a few inches thick; whereas soil formed on unconsolidated glacial deposits, especially wind-blown silts, are 5–10 feet (1.5–3 meters) thick and exceptionally fertile. These wind-blown glacial silts of the Midwest, as well as those of central and eastern Europe, Argentina, and New Zealand, all developed highly fertile soils. Should they be eroded, as has already happened in parts of New Zealand, they cannot be regenerated under today's climatic conditions.

Differences in soil type are important to us in other ways. Because some soils are more permeable and porous than the unweathered rock or sediment below them, they will temporarily store water from rain or melting snow, allowing it to infiltrate gradually through the less permeable materials on which they lie. These soils thus tend to reduce flood peaks and increase the recharge of the groundwater reservoir. Other soils, however, are less permeable than the underlying materials; consequently, they tend to promote ponding of water, flooding, or erosion, depending on their topography.

Soils and erosion.   Recognizing, then, the value of soils and the important role that geologic processes have played in their formation, we ought to note that erosion is a most serious threat to their preservation. Erosion has been wasting the land long before the advent of human beings; the Grand Canyon is one marvelous example. Man, however, has greatly accelerated the natural rates of erosion in many parts of the world by clearing forests, growing open-tilled crops, and exposing acre after acre of loose soil during construction and mining. Studies conducted by the U.S. Soil Conservation Service on four plots of ground of identical area and slope revealed that about 63 metric tons of soil per acre were eroded annually from fallow land and land planted with corn, as compared to only 80 pounds (36 kilograms) of soil eroded from grassland, and no measureable loss from forested land. Still greater losses have been measured on land where major construction projects were underway.

Altogether, nearly 3 billion metric tons of soil are eroded annually by wind and water from the fields and pastures of the United States.[1] Only about one-sixth of this eroded material actually reaches the sea; the remainder is redeposited along lower lying slopes, often damaging the soil below, or is deposited on river flood

---

[1] These 3 billion metric tons could cover about 1.5 million acres (600,000 hectares) with 1 foot (30 centimeters) of soil.

plains, in irrigation canals, stream channels, or reservoirs. Once again, we have a "resource out of place."[2]

Soils are clearly an important natural resource. At any one time in any particular place, the loss of soil through erosion may seem negligible, if apparent at all. But if we view the problem over a period of years and across an area as large as the continental United States, then soil erosion becomes a critical environmental issue.

Soils and construction.   Because of their inherent variability, the properties of soils must be considered when we plan construction, whether for a home, an industrial plant, or a highway. For example, a variety of soils can be encountered, often within short distances of each other, in building highways across the glaciated terrains of the Midwest. Soils formed on sand and gravel are usually quite stable for highway foundations because they can bear heavy loads and drain rapidly. At the other extreme, soils with high organic content, such as peat, have virtually no strength, but compress and squeeze outward when heavy loads are placed on them. Peat is also subject to rapid erosion, especially by wind, when it is drained. In fact, peat is such an undesirable foundation material that it is usually removed entirely and replaced with a more stable fill whenever a major highway has to be built over it.

Soils and minerals.   Besides serving as a substrate for growing food or as a foundation for construction, some soils are also sources of minerals. Most of the world's aluminum, and much of its iron, manganese, and nickel, come from "fossil soils" that formed under conditions of severe chemical weathering in tropical climates. The warm and wet climate of the tropics results in leaching of potassium, calcium, phosphorus, nitrate and even silica out of the soil, leaving an impoverished soil that is a mixture of the insoluble oxides of aluminum and iron, along with some other impurities. Such soils, called laterites, are characteristically yellow or reddish

---

[2]These erosion rates are only accurate for the specific situations where careful measurements have been made within a small area. It is difficult to extrapolate these data on a continent-wide scale with equal accuracy. Nevertheless, the figures give a reasonable range of the sorts of erosion rates we might expect and their relative variation under differing conditions of vegetative cover.

brown, and their upper parts dry to bricklike hardness. The hard surface layer may be a few feet to a few tens of feet thick, and is composed of a cemented mass of hydrated aluminum, iron, and manganese oxides. Some laterites contain a sufficient concentration of iron to be mined as iron ore.

When laterites have formed from parent rocks rich in aluminum silicates and lacking in iron and quartz, bauxite, a complex mixture of hydrated aluminum oxides, is produced. Bauxite is the principal ore for aluminum, and in the U.S. it is mined in Arkansas and Georgia. These deposits did not develop under the present temperate climate; rather, they formed during a warmer and wetter climate of the Tertiary Period.

Land conversion.   Converting land with fertile soils into uses other than agriculture may rival erosion as the most serious threat to the depletion of this important natural resource. For example, the state of California, which is the leading farm state in the nation based on its annual yield of agricultural products, is losing more than 90,000 acres (more than 36,000 hectares) of farmland each year to suburban expansion, highways, airports, and industry. Between 3,000,000 and 3,500,000 acres (1,214,000 and 1,416,000 hectares) of farming land have already been converted to nonagricultural use (more than 3 percent of the total area of the state). At the same time, millions of dollars are being spent to make semiarid lands suitable for farming by elaborate irrigation projects. As farmland acreage shrinks in California and elsewhere, production has to be increased in the remaining areas; often this means heavy doses of fertilizer and pesticides to force greater productivity out of the land and to minimize crop losses caused by pests.

NATURAL HAZARDS

With natural hazards, we have a somewhat different sort of environmental issue. We tend to ignore their threat to human lives and property because some processes (such as earthquakes, landslides, volcanic eruptions, tsunami, or floods), although potentially devastating, are sufficiently rare on our short human time scale that the threat is judged to be simply a "random act of nature" against which we cannot expect to protect ourselves. Yet we regularly hear of a natural disaster taking a great toll of lives and property in some part of the world. The recent death of 300,000 persons in East Pakistan (now Bangladesh) when the Ganges Delta flooded is an example of a serious natural hazard. In terms of human lives lost, this was one of the worst natural disasters the world has known. The severe 1964 Alaska earthquake took 130 lives and caused one-third of a billion dollars in damage. Even the "moderate" 1971 quake in San Fernando, California, resulted in 64 deaths and more than half a billion dollars worth of damage. And an even more recent disaster was Hurricane Agnes (1972), which wrought over $1 billion damage and took many lives in some of our most populous eastern states. The rain, to be sure, was a meteorological phenomenon, but the damage came mostly from flooding rivers escaping their customary confines—a strictly geologic process.

earthquakes

As serious as the Alaska and San Fernando earthquakes were, they would have been far more devastating if they had occurred in more densely populated urbanized areas, such as San Francisco or Los Angeles, during work and school hours. In that event, the loss of life would have been measured in the thousands, and the property losses in billions of dollars (Figure 4-5).

Fortunately, major earthquakes such as the San Francisco 1906 earthquake are rare events. In a particularly earthquake-prone region, large earthquakes have occurred at intervals no more frequent than several decades. The period immediately after an earthquake has been, historically, the time of least risk. However, this is also the time when afflicted areas place stringent restrictions on building practices. As decades pass without a serious earthquake, there is an unfortunate tendency to fail to enforce the provisions of building codes designed to provide earthquake-resistant structures.

Study of the San Fernando earthquake indicates that the California building codes that were intended to provide protection against the more serious effects of an earthquake were not, in fact, sufficiently rigorous. Hospitals, schools, buildings providing emergency services, and key facilities for communications, transportation, food, water, and utilities must be designed to withstand

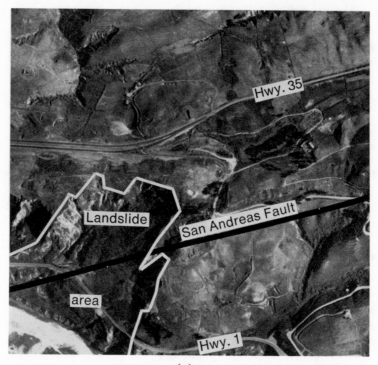

(a)

Figure 4-5. Aerial views south of San Francisco in 1956 (a) and 1966 (b). Suburban development straddles portions of the San Andreas fault zone (the dark line traces ground displacement from the 1906 earthquake). In the lower left is an active landsliding area being used (1971) for solid waste disposal. SOURCE: U.S. Geological Survey.

more severe ground shaking than the current building codes now require. The engineering lessons we learned from the San Fernando earthquake can also be applied to other earthquake-prone regions, all of which are well defined around the earth.

landslides

Other natural hazards affect us besides earthquakes. Landslides, often triggered by heavy rainfall (Los Angeles, 1968), by earthquakes (Anchorage, 1964), or by poorly planned housing and road

Hwy. 35

Hwy. 1

Landslide area

San Andreas fault

(b)

construction (Portuguese Bend, Calif., 1959) have long been a hazard, usually because of our propensity to put ourselves in the wrong place at the wrong time. Too often we fail to realize the potential danger of building on or near steeply sloping land.

A recent and tragic illustration of this human failing occurred during the 1970 earthquake in Peru, possibly the most catastrophic earthquake in the Western Hemisphere. The majority of the 40,000 deaths resulted from a tremendous, earthquake-triggered avalanche of debris that swept over, and largely buried, the cities of

Yungay and Ranrahirca, along with some smaller towns (Figure 4-6.) From 50 to 100 million cubic yards (38–76 million cubic meters) of rock, snow, ice, and soil traveled more than 9 miles, from a source high on the slopes of Huascarán Mountain, to Yungay, at a velocity of about 3 miles (nearly 5 kilometers) per minute. A particularly regrettable aspect of the tragedy was that Ranrahirca had already received warning of the potential danger, since it had been partly destroyed in 1962 by a much smaller avalanche of debris. Given the existing climate and topography of this part of Peru, such avalanches should be regarded as recurring phenomena.

tsunami

Another natural hazard is the tsunami that occasionally inundates islands or continental coasts of the Pacific Ocean. These "tidal" waves are caused by volcanism or earthquakes that disturb the ocean floor and generate waves that travel outward from the disturbance at great speeds, reaching enormous heights when they arrive in shallow water near land. Waves up to 115 feet (35 meters) high were observed on the Sunda Islands in the East Indies after the volcanic island of Krakatoa blew up in the Sunda Strait in 1883. These waves killed more than 36,000 people when they hit the coastal areas of the islands.

The Japanese coast is the most frequently hit of all Pacific coasts with, on the average, a wave 25 feet (7.5 meters) high being recorded in Japan once every 15 years. In 1946, a destructive tsunami, caused by a strong earthquake near the Aleutian Islands, struck the Hawaiian Islands with waves as high as 35 feet (10.5 meters). As a result of this disaster a warning system has been established in the Pacific region.

rare natural hazards

As part of our discussion of hazards we should mention some geologic events even rarer on a human time scale. The severe earthquakes of 1811–1812 in Missouri (New Madrid) produced damage over a far greater area than the better known earthquakes along the Pacific Coast. Yet the midcontinental United States is not generally considered a dangerous seismic area, inasmuch as only

Figure 4-6. Oblique aerial view of the debris avalanche that destroyed the Peruvian cities of Yungay and Ranrahirca, taking roughly 40,000 lives. The avalanche, set off by an earthquake, started about 9 miles (15 kilometers) up the slopes of the Huascarán Mountain. SOURCE: Photo courtesy of G. Plafker, U.S. Geological Survey. Credit for permission to republish is also gratefully acknowledged to the Seismological Society of America, in whose Bulletin this photo first appeared (Vol. 61, p. 522, 1972).

a relatively few, low-intensity earthquakes have taken place since the New Madrid quakes. Hence, earthquakes are given no special attention in the building codes of this region. Yet the seismic risk map of the United States published by the National Oceanic and Atmospheric Administration rates southern Missouri as having the same level of risk as the San Francisco and Los Angeles areas. Thus a repetition of the New Madrid earthquakes might well cause far greater damage and loss of life than all the previous Pacific Coast earthquakes combined (Figure 4-7).

Another similarly rare event occurred in 1902, when Mt. Pelée erupted on the island of Martinique in the West Indies. The nearby port of St. Pierre was completely covered by a glowing cloud of hot

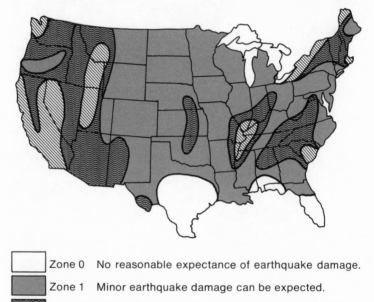

Zone 0   No reasonable expectance of earthquake damage.

Zone 1   Minor earthquake damage can be expected.

Zone 2   Moderate earthquake damage can be expected.

Zone 3   Major destructive earthquakes may occur.

Figure 4-7. Map of the United States showing regions of varying seismic risk. Note that areas around Boston, upstate New York, and the central Midwest have a potential for major destructive earthquakes equal to that of the California coast. SOURCE: California Division of Mines and Geology.

volcanic gases and ash which killed all but two of its 28,000 inhabitants. Yet this particular eruption was relatively a rather small one.

In 1943, volcanic gases, ashes, and cinders began erupting from a corn field near Paricutín, 200 miles west of Mexico City. By the second day of the eruption a cone had built up around the vent to a height of 250 feet; within a week it was 500 feet (over 150 meters) high, and in 10 weeks it reached over 1000 feet (more than 300 meters). There had been no historic records of volcanic activity around Paricutín, though the region contains volcanic rocks of ancient origin and extinct or dormant volcanoes with cones from 200 to 4000 feet (60 to 1200 meters) high.

There are many areas in the western United States that bear similar marks of recent volcanic activity. Deposits of volcanic ash that covered areas as large as half of the state of Nevada are not uncommon in the late geologic record of the west. About 2 million years ago there was deposited over the High Plains a layer of volcanic ash ranging up to a few feet thick and covering thousands of square miles. In Northern Mexico, two extensive ash falls are dated about 1½ million years ago. As the Paricutín eruption indicates, we might expect renewed volcanic activity somewhere in this general area. Volcanism that produces explosive emissions of gas and ash would result in the widest regional effects.

responding to hazards

An obvious way to avoid the hazard posed by a large-scale geologic phenomenon is to prevent high population density in the threatened area. There are, however, already large concentrations of people in many areas where such phenomena are likely to occur. Part of the attraction for people settling in a region near a natural hazard is often the resulting spectacular scenery or varied topography of the landscape. Consider, for example, the coast of California, where the active and major San Andreas fault is located. It is unreasonable to expect people to leave a region merely because it has been identified by geologists as being subject to a geologic hazard. What can and should be done to protect human life and property is inform the public of the nature of the hazard, indicate how different sorts of construction might best withstand the hazard, suggest the most probable time scale over which the hazard is likely to occur, and define low-risk areas where people could be encouraged to settle in the future.

CONSEQUENCES AND IMPLICATIONS

Given our understanding of the limits of the earth, we can make the following conclusions.

• Growing demands for nonrenewable natural resources cannot be met indefinitely. Large-scale recycling of many materials must take place eventually. Much of our solid- and liquid-waste disposal problems could be greatly reduced if we would recycle these wastes. Many pollutants might be better considered as "resources out of place."

• When recycling of wastes is not feasible, proper waste disposal requires thorough understanding of the disposal site's geology and hydrology to guarantee human safety and to preserve the natural environment. Radioactive wastes have special requirements all their own because of the great danger they pose to life and the very long time (sometimes thousands of years) they must be kept out of the biosphere.

• Soils are especially vulnerable to greatly increased erosion from careless land use. In a hungry world we must conserve valuable farmland as well as protect our forests and grasslands. Even though erosion rates seem so slow as to be "negligible," productive land can become a wasteland through poor management in a few generations or less.

• Natural earth processes occurring at irregular intervals, as they have for eons in earth history, become "hazards" when humans ignore them and settle in the "hazardous" areas where they occur. We must learn to recognize these processes and to avoid settling too near them, or, if we must live close to them, adjust our construction and our activities so that their threat to human life and property is minimized.

If we are to live harmoniously on "spaceship Earth," we must come to understand it: We have to recognize the limits to its bounty and the nature of the forces working on it. If we don't, life will become increasingly perilous for us and our posterity.

5

"... speak to the earth and it shall teach thee..."

Job 12:8

In our brief discussion of the earth and human affairs, we have emphasized the following ideas.

• The earth's resources are limited. They are either nonrenewable (as with fossil fuels and most metals) or renewable (as with water), if utilized at rates that are slower than their rates of regeneration. The lifetime of nonrenewable resources can be significantly extended by large-scale recycling programs or occasionally by substituting a more abundant material for a scarce one. Natural regeneration rates of renewable resources can be accelerated by human intervention, provided that such intervention does not introduce additional environmental problems. For example, water-treatment plants can "renew" waste water faster than natural processes, thus providing good quality water in quantities not possible otherwise.

• The earth has been, and continues to be, in a constant state of change. In no sense can we regard it as being in a timeless or primeval condition. The normal geologic processes of erosion and sedimentation, sea level rise and fall, mountain building and sea floor spreading, and shifting climates and habitats have kept the earth in a continuous state of flux for literally billions of years.

• In addition to the natural course of its dynamic evolution, the earth has been increasingly modified and sometimes irreversibly altered by human activity. If we are to continue inhabiting the earth, we will inevitably have a major effect on it. The critical issue is, therefore, *not* how to keep the earth from being influenced by humans, but how to harmonize our existence with the natural environment.

• The earth is essentially a closed system. The processes and phenomena acting upon it are cyclical and interconnected. Even though these cycles and interconnections are not always readily apparent, they are there, and must consequently be taken into account when we consider the impact of our civilization and technology on the natural world.

THE ALASKA OIL PIPELINE

"A large hot oil pipeline buried for hundreds of
miles in permafrost has no precedent."[1]

Perhaps the best way to integrate and emphasize some of the principles and concerns that we have outlined thus far is to look at a major environmental issue like the proposed construction of the Alaskan oil pipeline. Briefly, the proposal is to build a pipeline, 789 miles (1270 kilometers) long, from the edge of the Arctic Ocean on the north coast of Alaska, through the center of the state, across coastal plains, mountain ranges, rivers and streams, to the port of Valdez on the southern coast where the oil will be transported by ocean tankers to refineries in other regions of the United States.

---

[1]Final Environmental Impact Statement, Proposed Trans-Alaska Pipeline, Vol. 1, p. 93 (March, 1972).

Numerous questions are currently being debated, pro and con, regarding the impact of the pipeline and the importance of the oil. These questions include such things as the disturbance or possible destruction of the landscape and the flora and fauna; the vulnerability of the pipeline to damage or failure from floods and earthquakes; the problems of building the pipeline itself, as well as access roads, pumping stations, and airstrips, on permanently frozen ground; the claims of the native population—Eskimos, Indians, and Aleuts—to most of the land over which the pipeline would go; the significance of the oil in meeting future national petroleum needs; and the economic value of the oil in helping to balance our international accounts. Many of these issues are beyond the scope of this book. However, one particular aspect, that of the geologic nature of the proposed pipeline route, does interest us here. If the pipeline is to be built, what special aspects of Alaskan geology ought to be considered in its design, construction, and maintenance?

the route

In 1968, oil and gas were discovered in Triassic sandstones, 1 to 2 miles (1.5 to 3 kilometers) below ground, on the north coast of Alaska near Prudhoe Bay, several miles inland from the Arctic Ocean. An estimated 10 billion barrels of oil in these subsurface reservoirs cover an area the size of Massachusetts, and perhaps many billions more are yet to be discovered. The Arctic Ocean is frozen most of the year, so it is impractical to ship the oil by tanker from the north coast. Instead, a pipeline would have to be built to transport the crude oil from Prudhoe Bay southward across Alaska to the port of Valdez where tankers can operate throughout the year.

As shown in Figure 5-1, the pipeline will start near Prudhoe Bay and first cross about 125 miles (210 kilometers) of flat, treeless tundra to the foothills of the Brooks Range. This region of Alaska is referred to as the "North Slope" because the land slopes gently northward from the Brooks Range to the shores of the frigid Arctic Ocean. Along much of this segment the pipeline will follow the flood plain of the Sagavanirktok and Atigun rivers that flow northward from the Brooks Range into the Arctic Ocean.

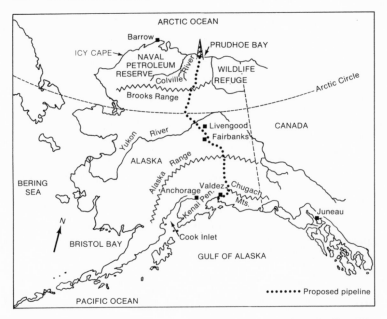

Figure 5-1. Map showing the route of the proposed Alaskan pipeline. The oil would be transported from oil wells on the north coast 789 miles (1270 kilometers) to the terminal facilities at the port of Valdez on the south coast.

The next segment of the pipeline, about 90 miles (145 kilometers) long, will cross the rugged Brooks Range, which is the Alaskan continuation of the Rocky Mountains. The pipeline will climb to an elevation of 4800 feet (1463 meters) at the Dietrich Pass. To this point the oil will be raised by three pumping stations, and then flow by gravity for the next 340 miles (547 kilometers).

On the south side of the Brooks Range the pipeline will cross a 350-mile (563-kilometer) wide interior plateau, a region of forests and streams. This section of the route includes the westward-flowing Yukon River and the city of Fairbanks.

The next segment of the route, about 75 miles (120 kilometers), crosses the Alaska Range, at close to 3000 feet (more than 900 meters) and then goes down toward the south coast. On the north side of the Alaska Range the pipeline will cross a major fault, the Denali fault.

After the Alaska Range, the route traverses the Copper River Basin for about 100 miles (160 kilometers) to the Chugach Mountains near the south coast. Rising and falling across this range for some 40 miles (64 kilometers), the pipeline will at last reach Valdez, about 10 miles (16 kilometers) farther on, located at the head of Port William Sound on the south coast of the state.

the land

The proposed route of the pipeline lies within several major physical environments. From north to south they are the North Slope, the Brooks Range, the interior Central Plateau, the Alaska and Chugach Ranges with the Copper River Basin lying between them, and the Port Valdez area. Each of these environments has peculiar geologic characteristics affecting construction and maintenance of the proposed pipeline.

Permafrost.   Both the world's polar regions are underlain by perennially frozen ground, or permafrost. Because of the below-freezing temperatures that prevail in these regions, moisture within the soil and bedrock exists in the frozen rather than liquid state. Approximately 85 percent of Alaska is underlain by permafrost that varies in thickness from 1300 feet (396 meters) near Barrow in the north to less than 1 foot (30 centimeters) in the southern part of the state.

In summer, when air temperatures are above freezing, the uppermost layers of the ground above the permafrost become warm enough for the ice to melt, but because of the permafrost layer below, the melted water collects at the ground surface, making a soggy, poorly drained landscape (Figure 5-2). The thickness of this uppermost, or "active," layer that freezes in the winter and thaws in the summer is controlled by the soil characteristics, the insulating effect of the vegetation mat, and the mean annual temperature.

In most areas of Alaska, rock and soil material have been frozen for thousands of years, extending well back into the glacial ages. In some places permafrost is more recent where new sediment has been deposited, where lakes and streams have changed location, or where humans have disturbed the natural terrain. The addition or removal of surface materials, such as sediment, water, or vegeta-

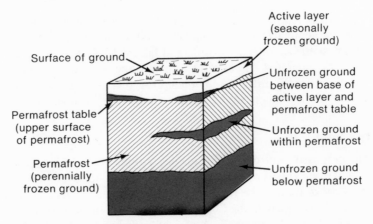

Figure 5-2. Block diagram showing permafrost lying below active layer and above unfrozen ground. The active layer may be inches to feet in thickness; the permafrost may be up to a thousand feet or more in thickness. The permafrost may include pockets of unfrozen material.

tion, changes the insulation of the ground surface so that the upper surface of the permafrost may rise or fall.

In a strict sense, permafrost refers to permanently frozen rock or soil, with or without ice. What concerns us here, however, is not icefree or dry permafrost but permafrost that has high ice content. The reason for this is that natural or man-induced thawing of ice-rich permafrost can result in dramatic changes of the physical properties of the rock or soil. The melting of ice within ice-rich permafrost causes the soil particles or rock fragments to collapse together because of the decreased volume occupied by the water as compared to that of the ice. Moreover, depending upon the slope of the land, the water may flow away from the thawed site by gravity. The change in volume and water flow often cause irregular subsidence of the ground, liquefaction and flowage of soils, and alterations in surface water drainage (Figure 5-3).

In building the proposed pipeline complex the insulating layers of the ground above the permafrost inevitably will be modified. Even the simple disruption of the vegetative mat of the ground by a vehicle destroys the insulating layer, and could cause melting and subsidence of the land. What in winter may be a hard, frozen roadway, becomes in summer an impassable muddy track (Figure 5-4).

Figure 5-3. Gravel road in Alaska showing severe irregular settling of the ground resulting from permafrost thawing below. Uneven distribution of ice within the permafrost caused the differential subsidence of the land along the roadway. SOURCE: U.S. Geological Survey, Professional Paper 678)

Figure 5-4. A road on the North Slope formed originally in winter on the frozen ground surface. After the spring thaw, the road has become a muddy ditch. Disruption of the insulating active layer has caused thawing of the underlying ice-rich permafrost resulting in a water-logged, poorly drained surface. SOURCE: U.S. Geological Survey.

Earthquakes and faults.   Alaska, with its rugged mountain ranges, active fault zones, and earthquake activity, is geologically the northwestern extension of the western United States. As noted earlier, the pipeline route will cross the Denali fault, a zone of fracture where ground dislocation occurred in Holocene time with total horizontal movements of about 1000 feet. Within the estimated 30-year lifetime of the pipeline, significant movement may again occur. But when such movement might occur, and how great the ground displacement might be, is impossible to predict.

The Chugach Mountains along the southern part of the state are extremely tectonically active, and faults are undoubtedly present there. Detailed geologic field mapping and studies of microearthquake activity will be necessary in this area to delineate these faults. Other faults have been mapped in the area between the Yukon River and Fairbanks in the Central Plateau, but we do not know whether they actually intersect the pipeline route or what their activity might be.

Ground shaking from earthquakes also occurs in Alaska. Such shaking causes landslides as well as liquefaction of water-rich soils and sediments. Geologic studies indicate that any point along the southern two-thirds of the pipeline route could experience an earthquake with a Richter magnitude of 7 or more. (In 1937 the area southeast of Fairbanks experienced a 7.3 magnitude earthquake. The 1964 Alaskan earthquake was magnitude 8.5, whereas the 1971 San Fernando Valley earthquake in California was magnitude 6.6.) One or more such earthquakes is almost a certainty during the 30-year lifetime of the pipeline.

Rivers and streams.   The route proposed for the pipeline crosses more than 50 major streams, the largest of which is the 0.5-mile (0.8-kilometer) wide Yukon River. In some areas the pipeline will follow river valleys, as in the north along the Sagavanirktok and Atigun rivers, usually being buried in the river alluvium. During the winter, Alaskan rivers and streams are frozen solid. At the annual spring thaw, these waterways flood, carrying away the accumulated ice and snow of the previous winter. Not only do water levels rise but the stream and river beds are deeply scoured by the floods. Where the pipeline is above ground, it must be sufficiently high to be protected from the flood waters. Where the pipeline is buried within the river and stream channels, it must be below the depth of maximal erosion. Pipeline plans call for construction across rivers and streams that could withstand the extreme sort of flood that might occur once in 50 years.

Construction of the pipeline also will alter surface water drainage in places where the pipeline is above ground, lying on a gravel pad. There will have to be culverts through the gravel pad to allow passage of surface water. Otherwise, the gravel pad will act as a dam and the ponds that could form would accelerate thawing of the underlying permafrost.

Sand and gravel.   Approximately 83 million cubic yards of construction materials, particularly sand and gravel, will have to be quarried along the pipeline route. A total of 288 potential sites have been designated to supply these materials, which will be mainly taken from stream and river deposits and upland sources such as alluvial fans and glacial sediments. Quarrying in watercourses will alter channel flow and cause siltation. Excavation of upland areas will change the slope of the terrain, result in thaw areas underlain by permafrost, and increase local erosion. Special precautions will have to be taken to leave the land after quarrying in a condition that would minimize these effects.

Marine environment.   Terminal facilities at the south end of the pipeline at Valdez will have to be built to handle the 600,000 barrels of oil arriving daily (at peak production this will increase to 2,000,000 barrels per day). Valdez lies at the northern end of Port William Sound. This deep-water, icefree port is part of a larger coastal zone that runs from the tip of the Aleutian Islands in the west to California in the southeast. This area, which rims the Gulf of Alaska, supports a great variety and abundance of marine life including fish, especially salmon and herring, shellfish, seabirds, and marine mammals such as sea otters, whales, and seals.

The harbor where tankers will take on the oil is relatively sheltered; thus, no special precautions for storms will be necessary. The threat of tsunami, however, is more serious because of the susceptibility of the area to earthquakes. The enormous waves generated by earthquakes could seriously damage the port's large oil tankers and petroleum handling facilities. However, the storage tanks will be above the level of the tsunami generated by the 1964 earthquake.

We have touched on only the highlights of the physical environments along the route of the proposed pipeline and suggested some
general problems that might result from the impact of the pipeline
complex on the natural environment. Some of the problems we
have posed become clearer after we describe the construction of the
pipeline.

the structure

The proposed pipeline will be constructed from special steel pipe,
48 inches (122 centimeters) in diameter and with walls ½ inch (1.2
centimeters) thick. Pipe lengths 40–60 feet (1.2–1.8 meters) long
will be specially welded and coated on the outside to prevent
corrosion when buried. Where placed above ground, the pipe will
be insulated with plastic foam and covered with thin metal sheath-
ing.

The temperature of the oil as it comes out of the ground will be
57°C and will be kept at about that value because pre-cooling
would be costly, the oil would become very viscous at lower temperatures and more difficult to pump, and at too low temperatures
thick waxy deposits would form inside the pipe.

The preferred method of construction is to bury the pipeline in
a trench to protect it from vandalism, keep it out of the way of
animals, maintain an even temperature within the flowing oil, and
minimize construction costs. However, because of the presence of
ice-rich permafrost that becomes unstable when thawed, the pipeline will have to be above ground almost half the route, where it
could be carried either on a gravel pad or on vertical steel supports.

Underground construction.   For roughly 312 miles (502 kilometers) of the route (39 percent) the pipe will be buried as most oil
pipelines are. Conventional burial, as this type of construction is
called, is within a trench, 6 feet (1.8 meters) wide and 8 feet (2.4
meters) deep, with the pipe surrounded by packing material to
prevent damage from bedrock, loose debris, and backfill. A cap or
crown of fill at the top of the trench is added to compensate for any
anticipated settlement of the backfill (Figure 5-5).

Conventional burial will be used where the ground is bedrock or
well drained sediment. Burial will also occur where thawing of

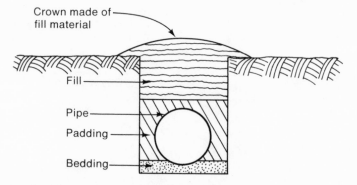

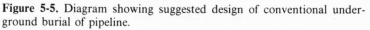

Figure 5-5. Diagram showing suggested design of conventional underground burial of pipeline.

permafrost would not result in too great subsidence or flowage of materials away from the pipe, which would leave the pipe unsupported and liable to rupture.

Special pipe burial will be required along about 70 miles (113 kilometers) or 9 percent of the route in areas where thawing of the permafrost must be minimized or prevented altogether. In this case the pipe may have an insulating layer surrounded by a special fluid that absorbs the excess heat from the oil. In the north, this technique is expected to prevent permafrost thaw. In the south, it has been suggested that special, refrigerator-like condensers be added that would extract extra heat from the soil and rock around the pipe and transfer it to the atmosphere (Figure 5-6).

Surface construction.   In many sections of the proposed route, burial below ground would make the ground unstable by the thawing of permafrost. In these areas the pipe will be laid on a gravel pad, up to 6 feet (1.8 meters) thick, that will act as an insulating layer (Figure 5-7). The pipe will be set out in a slight zig-zag pattern to permit thermal expansion and contraction without unduly straining the pipe. The pipe itself will be heavily insulated to prevent too much cooling that would make the oil too viscous to move. About 154 miles (248 kilometers) or 19 percent of the pipeline will be supported on gravel.

In some areas where gravel is unavailable, where slopes are too steep, or where there might be too much settling of the ground

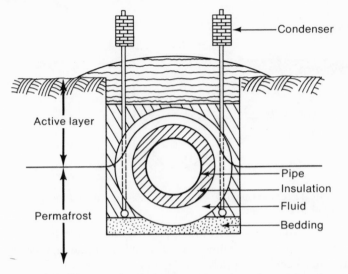

Figure 5-6. Diagram showing suggested design of special underground burial of pipeline where ice-rich permafrost must not be allowed to thaw. Pipe is insulated and has a special fluid around it to absorb heat. In the south, condensers will be added to withdraw heat and transfer it to the atmosphere.

below the pad, the pipe would be supported on steel piles 2–8 feet (0.6–2.4 meters) high and 60–70 feet (18–21 meters) apart (Figure 5-8). This technique would be used along 197 miles (317 kilometers) or 25 percent of the proposed route.

At river crossings the pipeline would be either buried below the river bed for 53 miles (85 kilometers) or 7 percent or carried overhead by simple spanning for 3 miles (5 kilometers) or less than 1 percent. The pipeline would cross the Yukon River, about 0.5 mile (0.8 kilometers) wide at this point, via a highway bridge. Where it is buried in river beds the pipe will have to be weighted down with concrete to prevent possible floating. The pipeline will cross 44 roads and will be buried at least 4 feet (1.2 kilometers) below the roadway. Of the total pipeline length, 435 miles (700 kilometers) or 55 percent will be buried and 354 miles (570 kilometers) or 45 percent will be elevated.

Additional construction.   Besides the pipeline itself, additional facilities will have to be built. These include a 361-mile (581-

kilometer) gravel road, 28 feet (9 meters) wide and 3–6 feet (1–2 meters) high, from the Yukon River north to Prudhoe Bay; oil field structures such as pumps, feeder lines, storage tanks, and crew quarters; 5 pumping stations along the route with 7 added later on;

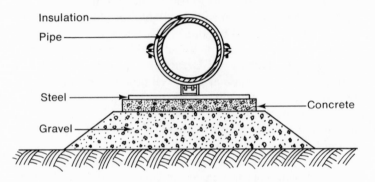

Figure 5-7. Diagram showing suggested design of surface construction of pipeline on a gravel pad.

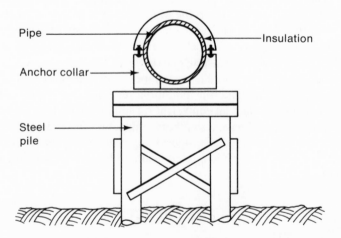

Figure 5-8. Diagram showing suggested design of surface construction of pipeline on steel piles. This mode of construction will be necessary when gravel is unavailable, when slopes are steep, or when too much settling would occur under a gravel pad.

7 airfields during construction, 3 of which will be permanent for pipeline maintenance; 900 acres (364 hectares) of terminal facilities at Valdez including storage tanks, pumps, oil-tanker berths and oil-loading equipment; and a telecommunications network, including 26 microwave towers, 30 feet (9 meters) high.

The oil fields at Prudhoe Bay will also produce large quantities of natural gas. A small fraction of this can be used for heating and energy to drive equipment. Initially, the excess gas can be reinjected into the oil reservoir. Eventually, however, it will have to be transported out because at peak well production there will be 1.5 billion cubic feet (43 million cubic meters) of gas per day, and this will be too much to reinject. (State law prohibits burning the gas at the wells to get rid of it because this wastes a valuable natural resource.)

A gas pipeline using the same corridor as the oil pipeline is not planned because of the high cost of liquefying the gas at Valdez for tanker shipment. Also, tanker activity in the port would have to increase by 50 to 100 percent and therefore require an appropriate increase in port facilities.

Although no formal proposal has been made, a gas pipeline across Canada—possibly up the Mackenzie River Valley—to Edmonton, Canada, would probably have to be constructed in the future if the proposed oil pipeline is built. From Edmonton the gas pipeline could join the existing one that comes into the midwestern United States. Even though a gas pipeline would run at a much lower temperature and the pollution resulting from a rupture would be far less than an equivalent oil spill, construction of a gas pipeline would still have a significant impact on the Alaskan landscape. Because no formal proposal has been made yet for a gas pipeline, it is not possible now to evaluate how great that impact might be.

THE IMPACT

From a geologic point of view, the proposed Alaskan oil pipeline would have several major effects on the environment. Sometimes this impact would be direct, as in the quarrying of construction materials; in other instances it would be indirect, as in oil spills resulting from pipeline rupture caused by landslides or earth-quakes, for example. In our relatively brief discussion of the Alas-kan pipeline, we indicate only some of the geologic problems related to its construction.

thawing of permafrost

Virtually any disturbance of the insulating layer of earth above the permafrost will cause a shift in the position of the upper boundary of the permafrost. Vehicular traffic, excavation for airfields, roads, and the pipeline, and the emplacement of the pipeline itself and accompanying structures and equipment, such as pumping stations or vertical piles, will disrupt the natural equilibrium between the insulating vegetation mat, the active layer, and the permafrost below. Usually the effect of this disturbance will be to thaw the permafrost and increase the thickness of the overlying active layer. Where the permafrost is ice-rich, large amounts of water will be added to the active layer and decrease its coherence and shear strength.

Thaw halo.   The burial of the pipeline in permafrost will create a "thaw halo" around the pipe. Such thawing is unavoidable be-cause, no matter how well insulated it is, the pipe will radiate some heat. Where the permafrost is just below freezing, this small in-crease in heat would be sufficient to melt the ice in the permafrost. In ice-rich permafrost the thaw halo would be a watery mass of soil and rock debris. Unless the individual soil particles and rock frag-ments are in contact and mutually supporting, the thaw halo will have a tendency to flow with gravity, even on very slight slopes. If this flow is horizontal, moving supporting soil and rock away from under the pipe, the pipe could rupture. The thawed material accumulating downslope could, by its weight, create enough pres-sure to break the pipe there as well.

Differential settlement.   Even if there is no significant flowage of the thaw halo around the pipe, or of ground materials under other structures, the melting of the permafrost can cause significant ground settlement. As mentioned before, the volume of ice-rich permafrost is greater frozen than thawed. Thawing in non-uniform soils can thus cause settlement of the ground. The resulting ground warping puts stress on the pipe, damages roads and landing strips, and weakens foundations of buildings and other structures.

We need to know in detail how the permafrost is distributed to judge the impact of its thawing. Although permafrost is generally thicker and more prevalent in northern Alaska than in the south, local variations in soil and rock, topography, surface water, and vegetation make it very difficult to predict accurately how much thawing might occur in any one place. Careful examination and testing of the permafrost conditions throughout the proposed route are, therefore, essential.

earthquake activity

Alaska is geologically young and consequently tectonically active. Hence, it is subject to earthquakes of considerable magnitude. When an earthquake occurs the energy released deep in the earth's crust is transmitted to the surface and expressed by ground shaking and faulting.

Liquefaction and landslides.   Ground shaking by an earthquake can cause liquefaction of fine grained, water-rich, granular soil and sediment. The shaking rearranges the soil particles and sediment grains so the interstitial water flows out as the particles and grains move together. This makes the whole mass behave as a viscous liquid. When liquefaction occurs on a slope, however low, the liquefied soil or sediment will move downhill by gravity. As with the thaw halo, transfer of a large mass of liquefied material could place great stresses on the pipeline by accumulating above ground. If the liquefaction occurs within the material in which the pipeline is buried, the movement of material could leave the pipe unsupported or press too heavily against it.

Landslides occur when gravity overcomes the internal shear strength of soil, sediment, or rock debris, because the energy transmitted to the loose surface materials may be just enough to overcome this shear strength. Landslides can be triggered by ground shaking from earthquakes or when heavy rains saturate ground materials and reduce their shear resistance, which causes them to collapse downslope.

Frequency of landslides thus increases when soils and sediment are poorly drained, as in permafrost areas, or when periodic ground shaking occurs, as in seismically active areas. The opportunity for landslides in Alaska is great, and this poses a danger for the pipeline because landslides could easily rupture it.

Faulting. Earthquakes can produce vertical and horizontal displacement of the ground surface during earthquakes. The resulting faults tend to be persistent and will move again from time to time. There may be long intervals when no movement happens and therefore a fault seems inactive or dead. Then, suddenly, an earthquake occurs and movement is renewed. A good example of this was the San Fernando earthquake when ground-surface displacement occurred in an inactive area while no movement was recorded along nearby, previously active faults.

Significant ground movement, either vertical or horizontal, across the pipeline route would clearly threaten the integrity of the structure. Special precautions, both in constructing the pipeline complex and in limiting oil spills should rupture occur, are required in areas where the proposed route crosses known or suspected fault zones.

topographic changes

One inherent feature of construction activities, however carefully pursued, is that they modify the existing topography. Alterations in the land slope and water drainage are particularly significant. These alterations, in turn, may displace stream channels, increase erosion, silt waterways, and produce landslides.

Besides the direct effects of these activities, there are indirect effects of other activities on land slopes that may become apparent only later. Permafrost thawing, for example, will be going on for many years after the initial emplacement of the pipeline; so its effects on the landscape will not be immediately evident. Thus, a settling or sinking of the land and landslides may later result from permafrost thawing and bring about significant changes in the topography.

Slope modification. Cutting and filling for new roads, landing strips, construction camps, oil field structures, pumping stations, and terminal facilities, as well as quarrying for sand and gravel, will necessarily modify the existing natural surface topography.

Artificial changes in a slope usually result in its becoming unstable and thus more prone to erosion and landsliding. In climates warmer than Alaska, ground slopes can be made more stable after construction by planting various kinds of vegetation whose roots bind the loose soil and rock debris. In the harsh arctic and subarctic climate of Alaska, this cannot be done easily.

Surface drainage.   Any topographic changes will, of course, influence the runoff of surface water. In some places, runoff will be blocked and ponding will occur. In other places, water courses will be diverted and land across which the water flows will erode. Again, as with slope modification, changes in surface drainage will not always be immediately evident upon completion of the pipeline. For instance, landslides and water from permafrost thawing may eventually result from construction; this could ultimately alter surface drainage. Increased erosion would bring greater amounts of sediment to the local streams and rivers. This process would cause siltation that might affect the fish and other wildlife using these watercourses.

oil spills

Environmental concern over the construction of the proposed pipeline arises not just from its impact on the physical characteristics of the land. Equal or greater concern is expressed about the pipeline's impact on the local animals and plants, not to mention the social and economic impact on the people of Alaska. In relation to wildlife, the major problem with the pipeline would be oil spills should the pipeline rupture. Such a threat to the integrity of the pipeline, as we have outlined, is mainly related to Alaskan geology: permafrost thawing, landslides, floods, earthquakes, and faults.

Current design of the pipeline includes a variety of gates and valves, automatically operated, to shut off oil flow if rupture occurs. These shutoffs are located on both sides of the Yukon River crossing, for example, where an oil spill would be especially damaging. Besides damaging the wildlife in and around the river itself, the oil would be transported downstream to the Bering Sea in which the Yukon empties. Similar shutoff valves will be located on either side of the pipeline where it crosses the Denali fault.

THE FUTURE

The first four chapters of this book have viewed the earth and human affairs in terms of the past and present. In this chapter we have briefly summarized a specific example of environmental concern over the immediate future as it applies in just one small "corner" of our globe.

Now, what of the longer and broader future? What positive steps can we take in our "human affairs" that will help us to live in harmony with this earth?

background studies

Background studies of earth processes are important as a basis for describing and interpreting the scale, timing, and present condition of earth systems of environmental interest before some planned environmental action is undertaken. Then the effects that a proposed action is going to have on existing environmental conditions can be assessed. Such an assessment might well suggest safeguards necessary to avoid or minimize harmful effects on the system.

What we have just said has already been expressed in the National Environmental Policy Act of 1969, which requires all agencies of the federal government to assess the impact *before* carrying out any actions. We are suggesting that impact studies be pursued whenever appropriate, not just in activities of the federal government.

For example, permits for construction of the Alaskan pipeline had to be obtained from state and federal authorities because most of the route would go over state and federally owned lands. These permits could not be granted until an environmental impact statement had been prepared that detailed the impact of the pipeline system on the physical, biologic, social, and economic characteristics of Alaska. The impact statement also had to include evaluation of proposed alternatives.

In March, 1972, a six-volume report was submitted by a special interagency task force under the coordination of the United States

Department of the Interior. After analysis of the report, the Secretary of the Interior announced the decision to go ahead with the construction of the pipeline. At this writing, however, that decision has been challenged in the courts and in Congress by legislators, conservation groups, and private citizens.

environmental monitoring

Once some environmental action is taken, there ought to be monitoring programs that can provide data on the environmental effects of that action. No matter how thorough baseline studies and impact evaluations might be, significant, unexpected effects may still be produced. Therefore, environmental monitoring programs ought to be established to indicate the actual impact of an environmental action. These programs would also, no doubt, provide new data about earth systems which might further our understanding and thus maximize our future efforts in maintaining the natural environment. Monitoring programs ought to be maintained over long periods of time so that long-range effects can be properly predicted. The recently developed ERTS spacecraft—earth resources technology satellite—is a major step forward in this regard. Television cameras and sensing devices aboard the unmanned spacecraft will take pictures and record data from the whole planet's surface and relay the data back to earth. This information will be useful to scientists, including agriculturists, geologists, and oceanographers, in monitoring earth processes and detecting significant changes.

In the case of the Alaska pipeline, the environment must be monitored all along the pipeline's route so any significant changes (incipient landslides, creep along faults, faster than predicted rates of permafrost thaw, ponding and damming of surface water) can be detected and dealt with before they damage the pipeline.

basic research

The relation of the earth to human affairs requires a broad understanding of earth processes and systems. It is not possible to know in advance what particular set of data or observations about the earth will be relevant to the solution of future environmental issues.

Even with many current environmental problems we lack the critical data necessary to evaluate adequately the impact of our existing interactions with the natural environment. Consequently, basic research about the earth must continue and flourish if it is to provide the essential framework of observations, concepts, and principles upon which the environmental impact studies can be soundly based.

The very nature of basic research is such that it will not always, or even usually, lead to discoveries that are immediately applicable. There is, of course, a kind of serendipity that operates in basic research, in which seemingly "useless" or "irrelevant" scientific inquiry turns out to have direct and important application.

Basic research should include inquiry not only into the nature of earth processes but also into the history of those processes; for the earth's present condition is the result of a long and varied evolutionary development. If we are to understand how an earth system operates, we may need to know both the present processes at work and how that system will change in the future—with or without human intervention.

As an example, geologic field parties have been studying Alaskan geology for many years, for the most part simply as an exercise in basic research. It now turns out that these studies have crucial importance in understanding the impact of an oil pipeline in this region. The problems posed by permafrost and earthquake activity could not have been fully evaluated, nor engineering solutions suggested, without this earlier basic research.

education

We believe that the issues we have discussed are sufficiently urgent that all citizens should have some minimal awareness of them. Continued efforts should be made to see that students are introduced to them at every educational level: grade school, high school, and college. The teaching of the earth sciences from a "human affairs" point of view is most reasonable and feasible.

We might ask, in the context of the Alaskan pipeline, how many citizens realized the significant relation between Alaskan geology and the pipeline. Even today, most popular accounts emphasize the impact of oil spills on wildlife and fail to indicate that the greatest potential for oil spills is closely linked to the nature of geologic processes and phenomena found in Alaska.

government

If we view government, whether local, state, or federal, as something we create to serve the needs and aspirations of our society, then it seems clear that government, too, plays a role here. Knowledge of the earth ought to be available at all governmental levels where environmental concerns are likely to come up for consideration. We must find ways for reliable, complete, and understandable information to be efficiently and promptly provided for persons in government and the public at large.

suggestions for further reading

There are a great many books available today that treat various environmental issues. The following, however, seem especially relevant to the theme of "the earth and human affairs."

Man's Impact on Environment, T. R. Detwyler (McGraw-Hill, New York, 1971). Collection of reprinted papers considering various impacts humans have on their environment, including atmosphere and climate, the waters, land and soils, and the spread of some organisms and the destruction of others. Each article has a list of references.

Environmental Geology, P. T. Flawn (Harper & Row, New York, 1970). Geology as it relates to "conservation, land-use planning, and resource management." The concluding chapter, which includes a large colored geologic map, illustrates the concepts and principles developed in the book as applied to the example of Austin, Texas.

Design with Nature, I. L. McHarg (Natural History Press, New York, 1969). Aesthetics and other human values brought to the question of how to live harmoniously with nature. Specific examples include the greater metropolitan areas of Philadelphia, Baltimore, and Washington, as well as Staten Island, N.Y., and the Potomac River Basin.

Man's Impact on the Global Environment, Massachusetts Institute of Technology (The MIT Press, Cambridge, Mass., 1970). Definition, discussion, and suggestions for remedial action regarding environmental problems of worldwide scope. A technical treatment containing important scientific concepts and quantitative data; many interesting references.

Resources and Man, National Academy of Sciences (W. H. Freeman & Co., San Francisco, 1969). Collection of papers analyzing current demand and future prospects of several important resources, including food from the land and the sea, mineral resources from the land and the sea, and energy resources. There are also papers discussing the human ecosystem and U.S. and world population trends.

Earth Resources, B. J. Skinner (Prentice-Hall, Englewood Cliffs, N.J., 1969). Brief review of the geology of metallic and nonmetallic minerals as well as water and energy resources. Indicates which minerals and fuels are abundant and which are scarce; also which are nonrenewable and which are renewable or recyclable.

The Biosphere, Scientific American (W. H. Freeman & Co., San Francisco, 1970). Series of articles by specialists discussing various cycles within the biosphere, including energy, water, carbon, oxygen, nitrogen, and minerals, as well as treatment of human production of food, energy, and materials as a process within the biosphere. Well illustrated and highly informative.

Man, Nature, and History, W. M. S. Russell (Natural History Press, New York, 1969). A fascinating account of the historical dimensions of the environmental crisis. Discusses human impact on the environment during Paleolithic, Neolithic, and Medieval Ages especially. Clearly demonstrates that environmental problems are not just the result of the twentieth-century Industrial Age.

postscript

Why—and how—this book came to be written should be of interest to many readers, who must be unaware of the metamorphoses it has undergone. Surprisingly, what started out to be a committee report for a small, select profession has become a book to be read (we hope with profit) by all concerned citizens. How has this come about?

In late 1968 an *ad hoc* committee, chaired by John C. Maxwell, at that time head of Princeton's Geology Department, was appointed by the National Academy of Sciences to recommend whether or not the geological sciences should be the subject of a study and survey similar to those made earlier by the Academy for the benefit of such fields as astronomy, physics, chemistry, and biology. In bureaucratic terms, the *ad hoc* committee was charged with "making a feasibility study."

In the following year the *ad hoc* committee reported that a survey of the state of the geological sciences would indeed be timely, and provided an extensive list of topics deserving attention —ranging from waste disposal to defense, and from geologic hazards to "other celestial bodies." Accordingly, Dr. Philip Handler, president of the Academy, appointed a Committee on the Geologic Sciences, composed initially of John Borchert, Ian Campbell (chairman), Richard M. Doell, John C. Maxwell (vice chairman), Siegfried Muessig, Clyde Wahrhaftig, and M. Gordon Wolman. Maxwell, Muessig, and Wolman had all been members of the preceding *ad hoc* committee. Cyrus Klingsberg, of the Academy staff, became executive secretary of the committee. Some months later, Muessig had to drop out because of increasing company responsibilities, and Delos Flint was appointed. A short time after that, Robert Bergstrom and Léo Laporte were added, completing the committee roster.

At the very first meeting of the committee we recognized that to carry out the full assignment proposed by the *ad hoc* committee would be an impossibility, in view of the limitations of time and budget under which the new committee would have to operate. We were well aware, by way of comparison, of the extensive report on geology and the mineral industry just then nearing completion under the auspices of the Research Council of Canada. This notable accomplishment had been staffed by several full-time personnel (we would have one part-time executive secretary), had involved dozens of committees and working groups (we had only ourselves), and had been over three years in the making. We could not hope to emulate that. Even more obvious was the fact that it would be virtually impossible to provide an adequate analysis of all the topics initially recommended by the *ad hoc* committee and at the same time comply with the recommendation that this be "the work of a single small committee and result in a single succinct document."

Recognizing that, in one sense, we were licked before we started, there were times when the Committee on the Geological Sciences came perilously close to giving up. But always some optimistic soul prevailed, and eventually we turned from concern with what we could not do to considering how we might best narrow the focus of our assignment to something we might reasonably accomplish. We reviewed our charges, and it seemed that the *ad hoc* committee wanted most to emphasize geology as it related to human affairs.

After much discussion, we agreed to do just that. Outlines were made, and remade, and revised. Writing topics were assigned. Manuscripts came in and were exchanged. The committee met to criticize, to edit, to revise, to curtail, to embellish, and to meet again! Better to organize the growing mass of manuscript, some members were assigned chapter responsibilities: Maxwell and Campbell on Chapter 1, Laporte on Chapter 2, Wolman on Chapter 3, Bergstrom on Chapter 4, Campbell and Wolman on Chapter 5. These men have carried the bulk of manuscript preparation. Yet decisions as to what should be included or excluded, what should go into this chapter or that, were for the most part settled in group discussion by the chapter editors. Even the choice of a word was in some instances decided by majority vote. Truly, the text of this manuscript has become an example of the democratic process! And, in the course of the various reorganizations and exchanges of material between the chapter editors, the individual chapters became so blended that they no longer strongly bore (as they once had) the imprint of any one man's writing style.

We had earlier decided that our efforts would have greatest value if they were aimed not at our professional colleagues, but at the "intelligent citizen," for, as had been pointed out by the *ad hoc* committee:

> new developments in and potential applications of the geological (and geophysical) sciences are essentially unknown to the public, the Congress, the Executive, and even to members of the earth science professions.

Of these august categories, we felt that the public not only had the most need to know, but also in the long run was in the best position to influence the applications of geology to human affairs. But we recognized our limitations; we were professionals trying to write for a lay audience, and we knew we might be falling far short (or to one side) of our mark. We sought the critical opinions of a few knowledgeable laymen and were both surprised and delighted at the enthusiastic comment we received. We began to take courage. Maybe our effort—to bring in readable form to laymen and students some of the important facts of life (geologically speaking)— might succeed despite its troubled beginnings.

Nevertheless, all of us on the committee knew, and our critics verified, that the manuscript at this stage "read like the report of a committee." This we knew would not do. What next? The dilemma was solved when one of the ablest and most dedicated members of the committee, Léo Laporte, volunteered to take the whole thing and make it "read like a book." For this enormous undertaking and its successful accomplishment no words can adequately express the thanks of the committee to our talented colleague. The least we could do was name him as "principal author."

Although the committee jointly and severally stands behind all the facts and opinions expressed, we must at the same time acknowledge the assistance (while absolving them of all responsibility) and encouragement we have had from many people. Herein only a few can be mentioned, such as Joseph W. Berg, Jr., executive secretary of the Division of Earth Sciences, NAS–NRC, who, with others of his staff, has been a constant source of assistance; the late

William T. Pecora, director of the U.S. Geological Survey (more recently undersecretary of the Interior), who met with us informally on several occasions and inspired us with his enthusiasm for the task we were undertaking; Elburt F. Osborn, vice president for research at Pennsylvania State University (currently director of the U.S. Bureau of Mines), who provided sage council when this was most needed; Harold Gertmenian and William H. Freeman, who read intermediate drafts of the manuscript and encouraged us to push ahead; and Howard Boyer, Jr., and Carol Verburg of Canfield Press, for their patient and helpful editorial assistance. To these, and the many who must remain unnamed, we express our sincerest gratitude.

So, after some two years of travail, the Committee on the Geological Sciences is pleased now to present what we, and others more objective than we, feel is a readable and highly informative discussion of some facts about our earth that deserve to be part of the knowledge of all men and women. May all who read it enjoy thenceforth the advantage of seeing many of our current problems in "geologic perspective."

Ian Campbell, Chairman

index

Boldface type indicates pages on which terms are defined.